Putt...g

Redundancy

Behind You

Putting

Redundancy

Behind You

A Life and Career Strategy

Sheila Cane and Peter Lowman

KOGAN
PAGE

Acknowledgements

To Mike Burge whose redundancy in 1991 was the starting point for this book and without whose coaching and encouragement it would probably never have seen the light of day.

And to all the following who contributed material and support: Deborah Protter, Sylvia Caplin, Christina Saunders, Sandra Andrews, Cindy Alves, Rowena Spence, Linda Maytum Wilson, Suzanne Mamourian, Peter Russell, Richard Beavan, Linda Jane Stanton, Douglas MacDonald, Ellen Balke, Tony Sofair, Roger Tweedale, Anne Hathaway, Val Lowman, Andy Carroll, Vanessa James, Jill Robertson, Keith Reynolds, Graham Yonwin, Bill Clarke and Mike Cooper.

We would also like to thank all those people with whom we have worked and who have helped us prove that it really does all work.

First published in 1993

Kogan Page Limited
120 Pentonville Road
London N1 9JN

British Library Cataloguing in Publication Data
A CIP record for this book is available from the British Library.

ISBN 0–7494–0992–4

Typeset by Saxon Graphics Ltd, Derby
Printed and bound in Great Britain by Clays Ltd, St Ives plc.

Contents

Part 4. A New Start

Introduction

This book has been written by two professional consultants both of whom were previously senior business managers with experience of being made redundant and being fired. We decided to write it because we believe that most outplacement agencies focus on what you have to do to get another job just like the last one. We have a different view. A holistic view. We believe that losing your job can be a miracle; it can provide the space to review and create just what you want from the rest of your life.

We believe that this is the only book that deals with completion before rushing to get another job. It is designed to help you create the job you want rather than just another similar job. It looks at your whole life rather than just your career. It is highly practical as well as being philosophical.

It doesn't tell you *what* to do; it tells you *how* to do whatever *you* decide to do. It helps, gives advice and supports you while you make it happen for yourself.

It takes you through the emotional shock of losing your job, supports you with structures for coping, helps you to rebuild your confidence, leads you through the process of creating a vision for what you want the rest of your life and career to be about, and then takes you through the steps necessary to help you find the job or start the business that makes your vision happen.

Part 1
The First Steps

1. Surviving the Crisis

How to be fired gracefully

To most people being fired is one of the most terrifying phrases in our language. Is it really possible to survive and, what's more, to handle it gracefully? Yes, it is.

We realise that you may well be reading this book after the event so we ask you to read this chapter without blaming yourself for what you didn't manage to achieve, but to recognise that there are some things you may be able to go back and resolve. For example, it may be possible to ask for a meeting with your manager or personnel department to discuss and negotiate an acceptable reference.

Remember that having to fire employees is one of the most dreaded activities of any manager. The manager is possibly even more upset than you are; after all, you will walk away – he or she will have to stay and deal with all the consequences. These include: recognition that he or she didn't manage you well, upset from other staff, additional costs of lieu of notice payments and employing a replacement. Having to fire staff is always an indication of poor management; at the least, of poor recruitment. So your manager may not do it very sympathetically.

- Don't panic.
- Listen carefully.
- Ask for specific reasons so that you are clear about everything
- Don't counter-attack if you can avoid it. If you are asked for your comments, put your point of view assertively.
- Make sure that you understand the arrangements and that you think they are fair.
- Check your legal position if necessary.
- Leave straightaway if possible.
- Do not go around the office saying goodbye.
- Leave the management to sort out the explanations.
- Ask a friend to clear your personal belongings for you.

Clarify what the future relationship will be. Will the company give you a reference or not? Negotiate a reference that is truthful but not damning, if possible. How will you refer to the firm in the future? After all, you chose to work for the organisation so you must have had respect for it. Negotiate what you will both say about each other. (Also, remember that if you are reasonable, the company is more likely to be generous about the financial arrangement.) You will be on much stronger ground in the future if you know what will be said about you. Even if you don't give the company as a reference in the future, it is likely that a potential employer will check back to see why you left that job. And if the reference isn't going to be good, you can think about how you will counter it.

Remember, there is no right or wrong. It just didn't work out. It is a waste of time trying to justify what happened. Remember that you were almost certainly partly to blame. From my personal experience of being fired, I should never have taken the job without asking a lot more about how the company expected me to work, but I was very pleased to be offered the job with a great title and salary (my ego gets in the way of my happiness yet again!).

Make sure that you get your P45 and a letter from the

company confirming dates and payments. Ask if the letter could include details about how you will be referred to. If it is possible, ask to take a negotiated written reference with you. You should reply to the letter acknowledging the details, regretting your leaving and confirming how you will refer to the company in the future.

If you are allowed to resign, all the better for your self-respect. Write a confirmation of regretful resignation including how you intend to refer to the incident and the company can reply with the above confirmations. However, if you do resign, it will affect your unemployment benefits. Some companies prefer you to resign because they will look better so, if this is the case, try to negotiate a better settlement to make up for the differences in lost state benefit. Weighing up the differences between the ego and the financial situation can only be an individual decision, but be careful not to cut off your nose to spite your face. Think it through; agree to leave immediately but ask if you can have another meeting the next day to agree details.

How to handle being made redundant

Being made redundant can often feel as bad as being fired. Very rarely is a whole company made redundant at the same time, so being chosen as unnecessary to the company's future can raise all the same feelings of rejection. So much of the previous advice is valid: don't panic; listen carefully.

Remember that managers dread making employees redundant. It implies mismanagement of the company, it causes upset for the remaining staff and it can cost a great deal of money.

There are some differences between being fired and being made redundant. In redundancy:

- You can get more money as a pay-off.
- You may have to work out some notice.
- Your function is being made redundant; it may have nothing to do with your skills or personality.

Listen carefully to what the management offers you. Negotiate for anything you feel you are entitled to. Many companies are now committed to a 'consultation period' which calls for as much notice of redundancy as possible, as well as allowing time to negotiate and suggest alternative actions after the formal announcement. Ask when the company wants to release you. Ask for time to confirm arrangements. Check your contract of employment. Check your legal entitlements. If you are a member of a trade union or professional association, ask for its help. The Citizens' Advice Bureau (CAB) can be a valuable resource. Sometimes you may be able to retain your season ticket; your company car may be offered to you at a reduced cost; medical insurance, pensions and other insurances, etc, may run for a period of time. Benefits you enjoyed as part of your employment may be negotiable.

Accept any career counselling support offered to you, whether it is from Personnel or from an outplacement service. Any help during this time is going to be of value.

Clarify the future relationship. Will there be some part-time work available? Would you be offered a position when/if the company becomes more profitable in the future? What sort of reference will they give you? Ask if you can have an open written reference before you leave.

If you are asked to work out a period of notice, treat it as a time of completion. Finish your ongoing work and leave all files, etc in an order that is easily understood. Ask if you can hand over your work to anyone else and do it willingly. Negotiate reasonable time off to start the process of life and career planning.

Try not to be a pain in the neck; it will upset your colleagues and add to the existing embarrassment, and in the long term it will not help you. The atmosphere in a company when redundancies are in the air can be appalling. Colleagues may feel embarrassed, guilty and/or relieved that it was you and not them. You will almost certainly be feeling somewhat upset that you have been chosen and not one of the others. Whatever the situation, the chances are that taking out your feelings on others will leave both sides feeling dreadful. What is important to you at this time is to leave with some grace and pride, so be as reasonable as you can. The way to empower yourself, and your former colleagues, is to accept the situation as gracefully as you can and complete your working relationships. If you have good friends among your colleagues who offer you genuine support, arrange to talk about the situation outside the office rather than during working hours.

Thank managers and colleagues for their support in the past and wish them the best for the future. They may have a very tough future if the company is not doing well. You at least know where you stand and may be able to look forward to a new life. They will be left in uncertainty which is always uncomfortable. It is possible that there will be opportunities for freelance or full-time work in the future: a good relationship and a helpful attitude now will help you to become the first choice.

If you are given a leaving party, be aware that it could be an emotional experience. Arrange for a friend or partner to collect you so that you do not have to travel home on your own. Also make sure that you collect your letters, cheque, P45, etc in advance and keep them safely. I have heard of several people who lost their redundancy cheques in the pub on their last day. It is *very* embarrassing to have to ring up on Monday morning to arrange to cancel and redraw them.

The whole company is being wound up

This is often a real shock. Most companies facing liquidation hardly admit it to themselves and the staff have no idea of the severity of the situation. There may be no waring at all.

If the company is made legally insolvent an Insolvency Practitioner will be appointed, responsible for dealing with commitments to employees. Payment of debts for wages owed, holiday pay, compensation for financial loss suffered because of insufficient notice (or none), can be claimed. You may also be entitld to redundancy payment. The Insolvency Practitioner wil normally arrange for you to fill in the necessary forms to claim these sums from the Redundancy Payments Service.

Go straight to the Unemployment Benefit Office and the CAB (or your solicitor, if you have one) to see what you can salvage. It can be helpful to arrange staff meetings where you can all air your views and work together to further your claim, if the company is in liquidation but not insolvent. Getting together with a group of people similarly placed is a very healing process. Appoint a committee to work on everyone's behalf to save time and money. This will help to relieve some of the negative emotions that are bound to be felt.

It is important to work as a group if you are in a position to make a claim on the liquidators. Seek legal advice on the likely outcome. It is important to find out what the levels of payment are likely to be so you can assess how much to invest in fighting your claim. Good legal representation is expensive; sharing the costs will obviously make good financial sense.

Sort out the basics

When you have received your P45 keep it in a safe place. You will need it when you have a new job or when you claim unemployment benefit.

Tax rebates
Your tax should have been correctly calculated in your final payment from your employer. If you believe that the tax deducted is incorrect, you need not worry because any overpaid tax will be refunded when you start work again. But if you want to appeal now you should do so immediately. Once you claim unemployment benefit, you cannot be refunded overpaid tax (except perhaps at the end of the tax year). You will need to contact your ex-company's tax office which is responsible for your records and any rebates.

National Insurance payments
From the day you register as unemployed, whether you are drawing benefit or not, you will be given NI credits. It is worth signing on for this alone.

How to register with the Unemployment Benefit Office
On your first day of unemployment, you should telephone to make an appointment with a new client adviser at your local benefit office (in the phone book under 'Employment Service Offices') even if you think that you are not eligible for financial help. Ask to be sent the 'Helping you back to work' booklet (ES 461) which you need to fill in to qualify for benefit. If you don't understand any of the questions or how to answer them, ask for help. (In some cases, where a large number of people are being made redundant from one site, Employment Service staff may be on hand to offer advice and answer questions in the two weeks before redundancies take effect.)

Your appointment will be made for a specific time, the interview will take about 30 minutes and you will not normally be kept waiting. Your client adviser will help you to identify the benefits to which you are entitled, tell you how to claim them and what local vacancies are available through the Jobcentre. He or she will also help you to draw up a back-to-work plan and issue you with a UB40 booklet that gives you advice about getting back to work and leaflets on the benefits available.

You will have to visit your local Benefit Office to sign on every two weeks. There is no way round this unless you live more than six miles away in which case you can sign on by post. Your signing on is a declaration that you have done no work in the last two weeks. You may also be asked to show what you have been doing to find a job. If you have done some temporary work during this period, your benefits will be proportionately reduced. If you are only doing a few days' temporary work, arrange this so all the days fall in one of your benefit weeks, and you will lose less benefit.

What benefits might you be entitled to?

Unemployment benefit
You will be entitled to this as soon as you stop working if you fulfill the following conditions:

- None of your final payment is in lieu of working out a notice period. If it is, you will only be entitled to benefit at the end of the notice period.
- You did not resign or get fired for misconduct. If this is the case, the details will be sent to the local adjudicator who will decide whether or not you are entitled to benefit, which can be suspended for up to 26 weeks. You will normally hear within one month.
- You are actively looking for work.
- You are available for work.
- Your Class 1 NI contributions are fully paid up for the last two years.

You should be entitled to unemployment benefit from the day you stop working if you fulfil the above conditions, whether or not your redundancy payment is more generous than the statutory amount.

You will not be eligible for benefit if you are not available for work. This includes illness, holiday or even attending a training course. Check with your adviser as in some cases he or she may be able to recommend payment. You are also not eligible for benefit if you are not actively seeking employment. We recommend taking a few weeks' break after losing your job in order to come to terms with the situation and give yourself time to think about what you want to do. If you have an in lieu of notice payment, this will cover you but discuss your position with your adviser. If you do not claim at the beginning of your unemployment, you will still be able to make a backdated claim. You should go to the Benefit Office to complete the claim form which will be sent to the local adjudicator for a ruling.

Additional unemployment benefit
This is available for your spouse if he or she is unemployed or has not worked. If you are living with your partner, but not married, the additional payment is only made if you have children.

EXPENDITURE AUDIT

EXPENDITURE ITEM	AMOUNT	CURRENT £ PM	ACTION	✓	IMPLICATION	REVISED £ PM
MORTGAGE	£650pm	£650	Pay interest only	✓	Mortgage will take longer to pay off. Lower outgoings	£495
COUNCIL TAX	£600pa	£50	Check if I can get a reduction?			
ELECTRICITY	£266pa	£22	Turn lights off etc	✓	More efficient	£20
GAS	£420pa	£35	Central heating on for less time	✓	Need to wear warmer clothes in cold weather	£30
FOOD	£200pm	£200	Buy less expensive items	✓	Our better and more healthy	£150
ENTERTAINMENT	£300pm	£300	Fewer outings to less expensive places	✓	Find out what to enjoy myself cheaply	£100
CLOTHES	£2000pa	£167	Buy only essentials	✓	May the cost spread	£50
MEDICAL INSURANCE	£80pm	£80	Cancel	✓	No access to private treatment	£0
TRAVEL	£90pm	£90.	Plan journeys carefully	✓	More effective use of roads	£40
	CARRIED FORWARD				CARRIED FORWARD	

Figure 1.1 *Expenditure audit*

Travel expenses

If you have been unemployed for more than four weeks, you may be able to obtain financial support for travelling to job interviews.

Supplementary benefits

Supplementary benefits are needs based and means tested as they apply mainly to people on low incomes and with minimal savings. The Benefit Office handles applications on behalf of the DSS and your local authority. To apply, you must fill in a lengthy booklet (B1). If you find this difficult ask for help. The Benefit Office will pass the completed booklet to the DSS who will forward the relevant portions to your local authority. Most payments to which you are entitled will be made together with your unemployment benefit through the Benefit Office. You may have to visit the DSS and your local authority as they decide whether the payments are to be made or not.

Because supplementary benefits are means tested your savings are taken into account. Unearned income may also affect your entitlements and debts are not offset against savings. Because the criteria change regularly, check with your adviser before applying. Take advice and consider your own financial position because, under some circumstances, it may be advisable to pay off all or some of your debts in order to be eligible.

Income support

This is a payment in addition to unemployment benefit and is needs based. If you qualify, you will be entitled to free prescriptions, free dental treatment and, if you are pregnant or have children under five, free milk.

You may be entitled to income support and other supplementary benefits even if you are not eligible for unemployment benefit. This applies particularly to people on low incomes and with minimal savings.

Sickness benefit

If you fall ill while unemployed you will not be able to claim unemployment benefit while you are unavailable for work, but you may be entitled to sickness benefit and possibly income support.

Mortgage interest
This is payable for people on income support. If the mortgage is in joint names, both partners must be unemployed or, in certain cases, not working more than 16 hours per week. For as long as income support is paid, 50 per cent of the interest will be paid for the first 16 weeks and from week 17 onwards all the interest will be paid. There is now a ceiling on this payment and in most cases the payment is made direct to the building society or bank.

Housing benefit
This is handled by the local authority and entitles you to a rent rebate if you live in rented accommodation and to a rebate on Council Tax. This rebate is normally given only if you are in receipt of income support.

There is a full range of benefits and these and the criteria for payment change regularly so check with your adviser. A claimant adviser is available to give advice on the benefits to which you may be entitled. You can ask him or her about local vacancies and seek advice on getting a job. You may find it convenient to meet him or her when you sign on.

All the staff are committed to helping you through difficult times but remember that they are often under enormous pressure so be as efficient and polite as possible. Make friends with them, become a joy to serve and it will pay enormous dividends.

Take charge of your finances

Work out a temporary budget. Decide exactly how much you need to spend each month on bills, mortgage, heating, etc. Add an average weekly cash sum for food, travel, etc, and a bit more for treats, and estimate a weekly or monthly sum. Does it balance with what you have coming in? If you have savings or a redundancy payment, work out how long you can live without running into trouble (see page 26).

You may have some monthly payments that you can afford to reduce or drop for the time being. Some people cancel items like medical insurance if they are out of work, but it is advisable to keep up home contents insurance. Remember that personal insurance policies may have a derisory surrender value, so take impartial advice. Try to look objectively at each item and weigh up the benefits against the costs. List each item, what it costs, what you gain from it and what the implications of cancellation would be. For example:

Item	Cost	Implications of cancellation
Phone	£30 monthly	Difficult to contact potential employers, etc
		Difficult for them to respond to letters, etc
		High reconnection charge in future

Another option might be a lock on the phone so that you can receive incoming calls but have a way of controlling the number of outgoing calls.

It is important to take control of your finances. Be honest with yourself and take your decisions responsibly. Often your cash will last much longer than you expect without causing undue hardship if you use it sensibly. This is an opportunity to learn the real value of money.

Visit your bank or building society manager. Ask for help if things are going to be tough. Check whether you have unemployment cover insurance. *Always* tell people that you are in trouble *before* you run into debt. Most big companies have advisers; for example, the gas, electricity and phone companies always try to help customers rather than cut them off, and some building societies may allow you to reduce your payments for a time. The CAB runs helpful debt advisory services that don't make you feel an idiot – they are not there to judge you.

If your financial position is very tough and you need to find paid employment immediately, please read Chapters 2, 3 and 4 on emotions and stress quickly before moving on to the practical finding a job chapters (Chapters 7–12). When you are back on solid ground, you may want to consider the longer term, in which case go back to the life and career planning section (Chapters 5 and 6).

Budget Planner

Financial position as at ....

Monthly expenditure	Now	Mininum	Action required
Rent/mortgage	£	£	
Council Tax	£	£	
Electricity	£	£	
Gas	£	£	
Telephone	£	£	
TV licence/rental	£	£	
Insurances	£	£	
Car	£	£	

Other regular payments, including standing orders:

	Now	Mininum	
	£	£	
	£	£	
	£	£	
	£	£	
TOTAL PER MONTH		£ _____	
Cash per week	£	£	
Food	£	£	
Travel	£	£	
Family expenses	£	£	
Clothes	£	£	
Going out	£	£	
Fun/treats	£	£	
TOTAL PER WEEK		£ _____	
Debts	£	£	
Credit cards	£	£	
Overdraft	£	£	
TOTAL		£ _____	

2. The First Few Weeks of Unemployment

Dealing with limbo

This is not going to be an easy time. You are in a life-changing situation, a transition between one lifestyle and another. You are in limbo. You will probably desperately want the new lifestyle to begin, but sometimes it isn't that easy. Usually we need to allow the old way of life to finish properly, to be complete, first. I was given these golden rules and have found them enormously helpful.

- Take your time; don't fill up every moment. Leave yourself some space to think.
- Arrange temporary structures for support (routines, timetables and plans), and remember that they are temporary. Consider them as scaffolding that can be taken down when the new, permanent structure is in place.
- Don't act simply for the sake of action. When in doubt, *don't do*.
- Recognise why it all feels so uncomfortable.

- Take good care of yourself; give yourself some regular treats.
- Explore the other side of the change. Look at both the positive and negative aspects.
- Find someone to talk to who will simply listen, without giving advice or sympathy (see Chapter 4).
- Find out what is waiting in the wings of your life. What kind of things are possible?
- Watch your spending. Use your new financial plan. There is a real temptation to blow some of the golden handshake but you may have to live off it for a long time. Limit your spending to what is really necessary (see page 26).
- Don't panic. It is going to be a shock not having a job to go to. Create a routine. Remember that what has just happened to you is going to be stressful, so take steps to minimise your reactions. Cut down on caffeine, alcohol and nicotine. Increase exercise and eat a balanced diet. Establish a good sleep pattern. Create at least one activity per day that brings you into communication with other people. Don't hide away from the world. Look after yourself.
- Divide your day into blocks:

  > First half of morning
  > Second half of morning
  > First half of afternoon
  > Second half of afternoon
  > Evening.

- Discover which are your most and least productive times and plan for them. For example, if early afternoon is a dead time for you unless you are active, use that time for exercise, shopping, etc. If the first section of the morning is by far your most productive, hit your desk as soon as you've washed and dressed. Find out what is right for you.
- Try to create gaps between each block; use refreshment and lunch breaks.

- Because I work from home, I generally have a bath at the end of the afternoon to distinguish between day and evening. Sometimes a day can seem very long without breaks and changes in activity.
- Here are some activities that you might want to plan for:

> Exercise – both frustration-releasing and stamina-building
> Spending time with your family
> Time with your friends
> Time with your business contacts
> Working on your plans for the future
> Researching short courses
> Reorganising your home.

I am a great believer in sorting out your home when you are in a difficult period. It may sound a strange thing to ask you to do but you are going to be spending a lot of time there so it might as well be really comfortable. I suggest that you clear out all your wardrobes and cupboards as a way of completing the past – throw out all the rubbish and make way for the new. Some people repaint their homes as a way of releasing stress (*any* activity is good for this). While you are painting all sorts of ideas come into your head and the whole place looks new and welcoming.

Remember, you can do what you want whenever you want to. You can go to the cinema in the afternoon and work in the evening. There's no one to tell you what to do or when to do it any more. It is up to you how you achieve your goals. Some people find that leisure facilities are much less busy and (sometimes) cheaper in the week than at weekends.

Remember to get support. Each item below will be a project, and self-employed people (you are now self-employed in working out what you want to do next) need personal coaches. Find a friend or family member whom you trust to talk your projects through with. (I find that someone to report back to is crucial. I am lazy and therefore put things off for ever unless I have arranged to keep in touch with someone about my projects.) You also need lots of encouragement.

Sometimes it is hard-going, so find a special person to share your weekly and daily goals with to help you succeed. This is a two-way process and he or she may even be in a similar position so you can help each other. But remember that it is support you need and not sympathy!

	Mon	Tues	Wed	Thur	Fri	Sat	Sun
7.00–9.00							
9.00–10.45							
11.00–12.45							
Lunch							
2.00–3.45							
4.00–6.00							
Evening							

Temporary structure: action plan

Decide on your own menu of activities before planning each day:

- Exercise
- Rest/relaxation
- Reorganising home
- Food
- Time with family
- Time with friends
- Fun time
- Treats for yourself

- Time to think about what you want to do
- Action on what you want to do (research, contacts, etc)

Being nice to yourself

When the going gets tough it is important to be nice to yourself. We need to look after ourselves very carefully. This means doing things that make us feel good, but not things we shall regret after, such as overeating, an alcoholic binge, or a shopping spree. Here are some suggestions:

- If the weather is good, spend some time outside. Read or plan while sitting in the sun.
- Play your favourite sort of music most of the time: music lifts your mood and will help you to avoid depression.
- Eat well (not necessarily expensively); buy all sorts of healthy fresh food that you find delicious. After all, you now have the time to shop carefully and cook properly, rather than rushing around the supermarket grabbing expensive convenience foods.
- I make baths into a ritual. I play music, light candles and fill the bath with lots of hot water, bath foam and add five drops of essential oils (different oils have different effects: the Body Shop has a range).
- Wear clothes that you feel good in: even if you are going to be in sweatshirts and jeans, wear your favourites.
- Always wash your hair, shave, etc, to feel good about yourself.
- If there's nothing on TV that you want to watch, get a video or play your favourite music while you read.
- Recognise that you are in control of your life. If what you are doing right now is not going well, reorganise your schedule and do something else instead.
- Go for walks, visit exhibitions – do all the things that you never had time for.
- Experiment with different creative activities – painting,

singing, writing, cooking, pottery, redesigning your
home environment. Discover what suits you.

- Learn new things. Maybe go to evening classes.
Volunteer to do different things that you have always
been interested in. There are lots of one-day courses
available.

- Spend time with youngish children. They are good at
bringing you back into the moment. They also allow
you to be really silly and have a great time.

- Remember to laugh. Have fun. Find out what is real fun
for you. This is also part of finding out who you really
are and what you want out of your life. This is the
beginning of life and career planning.

Completing the past

One of the steps required before you can start planning the
future is to complete the past. In order to look at the future,
we need to make sure that we are standing in the present rather
than the past. When our past is complete, we can be
comfortable in the present which allows us to look to the
future positively.

One of the difficulties faced by many people when they have
lost their job is to come to terms with the reality that this is the
way it is. For a while they are stuck in what should have been
and how unfair it is. We have all heard stories about people
who have lost their jobs and still leave the house at the same
time each day to avoid telling their family the truth. I know a
man who, when he lost his job, disappeared for three days
because he didn't dare go home.

So the first step is to recognise the truth of the situation: you
have no job right now. Once you are clear in your own mind,
you will be able to plan how to tell your family. Remember, if
they love you, they will support you. If you are living a
fundamental lie in your relationships, you have no relationships.

And don't forget the children. Most children are far more
aware than their parents think they are. If there is something

going on, they will be aware of it. If you don't tell them what it is, they will probably imagine that it is far worse than it really is. (If we don't know the truth, we usually invent a scenario that is like a disaster movie, don't we?)

When you are clear with your family, tell your friends. After all, they are not your friends if you are still pretending to be something that you are not. Don't live in the fantasy of 'it will all work out and people need never know'. They will almost always know that something is wrong and the trust between you and them will be damaged for ever. It is dangerous to live in fantasy. It is likely to cause a real crisis in the not-so-distant future. Get your feet planted firmly in the ground, in reality. You are going to need support and encouragement which you won't get unless you tell people the truth.

Part of accepting the reality is to sort out your finances. Living off credit in the assumption that it will soon be all right again isn't going to help. And it will quite possibly get you into far more trouble than you are in right now.

Completing the past often means a period of mourning for what is no longer in your life. The phrase that I like is: that was then and this is now. When you have completed the past you:

- will be able to think about it without anger or upset
- will have nothing more to say about it
- won't need to justify what happened
- won't feel guilty about it
- won't regret it.

Time is a great healer. You will almost certainly need to keep talking things through. I find that I write about events to help me clear things. There is definitely a period of debriefing to go through.

You will also need to recognise that there is nothing you can do to change what has happened. You will almost certainly have learned a great deal from the experience (if you have allowed yourself to), and without that experience you would not be the person you are now. So regret and wishing that it hadn't happened are a waste of time.

3. Rebuilding Confidence

After any career crisis, there is almost certainly going to be a drop in your self-esteem, a lowering of your self-confidence. We are conditioned, in our society, to be valued for what we *do* rather than who we *are*. We feel that we are valued for our status and status symbols. For example, not having a car suddenly may feel like a drop in our value. If people around you are reacting badly to this sort of drop in status, remember that it probably says more about them than about you. You don't need those people around you. You are more important than your status symbols and this chapter addresses this issue.

If you are without a job, it can be hard to answer when people ask you what you do. When you are without a job, and therefore not doing a job, it is difficult to continue the conversation. I know. I've been there.

Developing a positive outlook

When I was fired, I was helped by one of my supporters who only allowed me to wallow for 36 hours before announcing, 'Congratulations! This is the best thing that could have happened to you. You hated that job. Now you have a chance to decide what *you* want to do.'

We help people to come up with a phrase that they can use in these situations. For example:

'What do you do?'
'I've recently left a job where I wasn't happy and right now I'm planning to become a....'

Your *job* is evaluating, planning and implementing what you are going to do next. Each person will probably need to say something slightly different. It is vital that *you* are comfortable, so some alternatives might be:

'I'm planning my new life'
'I'm preparing to move to the country/another town'
'I'm going to retrain to become a ...'
'I'm working on what I want to do this time.'

It is important to remember

- You *are* doing something
- *You* are in control of what is happening
- *You* are living your life, not life living you
- This is about *you* not about what's wrong with the world.

When you are able to talk about what you are actually *doing*, you can start looking at who you *are*. Remember that not having a job doesn't mean that you have stopped being a great, exciting, valuable, talented human being (but just sometimes it feels rather like it!).

So start making lists about what a great and wonderful person you really are. It's great fun, it really cheers you up when it gets going, and it is all part of the career/life planning process that we will go into in more detail in Chapter 6.

I don't know when we lose the ability to be able to string together long lists of our qualities – somewhere at school I suspect. For an experiment, I once asked my five-year-old niece what she was good at and she unhesitatingly gave me a list that lasted 45 minutes and included such gems as 'I am good at loving people' – and she *is*! I was so impressed.

One of the reasons we don't do it often is that we feel

big-headed and vain. I have a theory that may help. In my experience people who know and are proud of their qualities look hard to find them and acknowledge them in other people. I think it is a socially valuable skill to be able to live from your strengths rather than your weaknesses, and to do that we need to know what our strengths are.

To create the sort of life and job that you want, you must value yourself, you must radiate your value to the world so people recognise that they want you in their lives/organisations.

I am a great and wonderful human being because I ...

Affirmations
When you've made your list, read and consider it very carefully. Often all these wonderful things don't feel like us at all! So start to use them as affirmations.

Affirmations are statements of what we want to be more of, rather than how we necessarily feel right now. Say them at set times of the day (morning and evening?) and listen to your reactions.

Say 'I (name) am ...' Repeat this five times and listen to your reaction.

Say 'He/She (your name) is ...' as if your friends are saying it. Repeat this five times and listen to your reaction.

When you start, the reactions tend to be negative, but after a few days we can begin to say, 'Possibly, maybe, could be and, even, yes!' Then we can start to *be* what we affirm more of the time.

A process that can be valuable when you are given a new quality you didn't know about yourself is to live it for a week or so. For example, recently Richard, a senior manager in a city institution, commented that I am very perceptive. So for a week I tried to remember that I was supposed to be perceptive and slowly I became more and more comfortable with this new quality.

Often people around us know more about our potential greatness than we do, so it is important to listen to positive feedback and become more conscious of behaving out of our strengths rather than covering up our weaknesses.

Projecting confidence

You can't get what you want unless you let people know what that is, and you certainly can't do that until you know what it is yourself.

If you want sympathy you don't need to be confident. But if you want help and support in finding what you want out of life, you need to be projecting that you value yourself, so that the world can begin to value you as much as it should.

The key is to radiate your value whenever you are in public. When you go out, stand straight and tall, look the world in the eyes, look good and feel good about yourself.

Image consultants can be useful here. They are often regarded with suspicion and have been associated with 'making people over' for television. But my experience of visiting an image consultant is that he or she can advise you about what colours help you to look your best, what styles of clothes suit you best, what shape of glasses, etc. I found mine very valuable, not least because now *all* my clothes go together and I don't have things in my wardrobe that I wear only occasionally. The advice of image consultants is usually only common sense, but they are objective and therefore tell you the truth instead of what your friends think you want to hear.

Wash your hair, shave, put on make-up, wear clothes that you feel good in whenever you go out. If you meet friends and ex-colleagues and they immediately start sympathising with you, you will feel that there is something wrong. Start projecting the excitement that a new life could give you.

There is a maxim which goes: Behave it, believe it, be it. This means that you may have to start consciously behaving in a new way before you can start to believe it – and then you will find yourself being it.

It works! There is something powerful about behaving in a different way which makes the whole world suddenly appear different. If you decide before you go out that the world is a wonderful place with everything you want available to you, somehow that is exactly what happens. It's called creating the world you want. We can look at it in many ways: if we expect life to be tough, it tends to work out that way. It is my (and many other people's) experience that if we expect life to be great, it will be.

So, how would you be if you were great and valuable to the world? How would other people appear if they were there to help you? Now, go and try it.

Look as if you are great and valuable to the world.

Talk as if you are great and valuable to the world.

Meet people as if they were a resource that will help you to get what you want. Treat every experience as an opportunity to learn and discover what you want. Smile, be happy, look forward to each moment. Treat each day as the first day of the rest of your life.

4. Managing the Stress

When we are involved in a major life-changing situation, we may feel that we have no choices. We may feel that we are at the mercy of the situation, that the world is running us. We often feel completely powerless.

This is not the truth. It is simply how we feel for a time. We always have a choice.

We have a choice in how we respond to any situation

Having a crisis in our career doesn't mean that we are failures or that we will never get another job. The key is to choose how you are going to respond to the crisis.

When early man became aware of a sabre-toothed tiger his body reacted instinctively in one of two ways: fight or flight. He instantly prepared either to fight the danger or to run away from it. Chemical responses poured through his body, his blood rushed away from his digestion to his limbs, his breathing changed to prepare for action.

We haven't changed much over the millennia. Our bodies still react in the same way to danger; we perceive that losing our job is as threatening as a sabre-toothed tiger.

What we have to do is understand what is happening in our bodies and find ways of releasing the chemicals safely. And we have to learn how to recognise the situation for what it really is. It is rare that we are in a life-threatening situation: what we are usually facing is an ego-threatening situation. It was not what we wanted; it wasn't what *should* have happened.

By identifying this inner conflict you can often reduce the stress that you are causing yourself – and by learning more about your own expectations you can react more calmly in the future.

Stress experts have known for a long time that we are disturbed by the view we take of a situation rather than the situation itself. In the first century BC a Roman called Epictetus noted that 'men are disturbed not by an event itself, but by the view they take of it'.

This is not to say that you should avoid feeling any uncomfortable emotions around a life-changing situation – that would be impossible. What we are saying is that having recognised the emotion, you can choose whether or not to allow it to stop you moving into action.

Once we have identified our 'shoulds', it is possible to consider other ways of responding to the event. For example, if you have been made redundant there may be many different ways of reacting:

Anger because you are out of a job

Upset because they are willing to be without you

Joy because you suddenly have lots of time and perhaps some extra money

Excitement because you can now plan a new future

Relief because you don't have to do a job you didn't like

Relief because you know your situation – end of uncertainty

Fear because you are responsible for what happens next

Privileged because you now have a second chance at your career

Resentment that your hard work over a long period was rewarded in such a way.

There are probably many more, and you may be feeling several of these emotions. But the point is, you *choose* which of these emotions you act on.

Situations don't make us angry or upset; it is the view we take of them that allows us to feel the emotions. So, *we* are responsible for our emotions, not the other person or the situation.

Someone to listen

We all need someone to listen. But when you have lost your job you may feel vulnerable and need support in order to see a positive way of responding. One of the most effective ways of releasing stress and uncomfortable emotions is to talk. But when you are feeling 'down' you may feel that you are imposing when you ask to talk to a friend. Turn the situation around. How would you feel if someone you cared for asked for your help when they were in trouble? Wouldn't it feel good? Maybe it is a gift to ask a true friend for help.

The difficulty is to find someone who will *listen*. Most of our families, partners and friends feel uncomfortable when we are unhappy. They try to make us feel better, they sympathise, they try to get us to 'snap' out of it, they give us advice, they tell us what to do next. But these things rarely work. They make us feel that it is wrong to be feeling the way we do.

A 'listener' will:

- not make judgements
- not give advice
- not take over the situation
- trust us to move on when we are ready
- not make a 'big deal' out of the situation
- accept the reality of our feelings without it being the 'truth'
- understand that talking helps us to diffuse the feelings.

So you need to find someone who you trust. Someone who you believe respects and cares for you as an individual. When you have identified a possible candidate, ask if he or she would be willing to help you and explain exactly what you want. Then allow that person the space to decide whether he or she can fulfil the requirements, and don't be upset if they feel unable to. Look for someone else.

You may want to ask the person to listen first and coach you afterwards. But before your listener moves into coaching, he/she should ask your permission. If you have asked them to listen and they want to help you move forward, they should ask whether this is what you want or whether you are ready to move forward.

For example:

I would like to ask some questions, would that be OK with you?

Coaching involves asking the questions that you are not asking yourself. Such as:

- Are there any other ways of looking at this?
- What didn't happen that has upset you so much?
- What do you want to happen out of all this?
- Can I help/support you in any way?

How to diffuse uncomfortable emotions

As we said earlier, it is impossible to avoid the uncomfortable emotions that come up in these circumstances; the key is being able to recognise them and then deal with them so that they don't block you from action. (If you try blocking them out, the chances are that they will lie low for a while, and then come up and hit you from behind, even stronger and more violent than they were before – this is dangerous.)

The two most common emotions are fear and anger. So let's spend some time looking at them and how you might start to diffuse them. The first step is to recognise the emotion.

If you are facing fear, try to look at what you are so afraid of and come to terms with it. My worst fear for years was being fired. Suddenly, it had happened and I had survived. I wasn't feeling great, but I was still here. I still had my family and friends. While I was reading various management books, I came across a piece by Tom Peters, the leading US management guru. He said that it is important to work in the right company for you, that even the most brilliant manager won't succeed in the wrong company. That came as a huge relief. I started to realise that I wasn't necessarily a disaster just because one company didn't want me. I held on to some of my earlier successes and the panic began to fade.

I also now realise that, at the time, I forgot that the company had originally chosen me at the interview so I can't have been such a disaster!

Another realisation was that having survived this crisis, it would never be as bad again. Major changes in our lives feel very threatening but once you've managed the first change, it gets much easier in the future.

Common emotions at this time are frustration and anger which it is helpful to start to dissipate. There are lots of constructive ways of releasing anger:

Beat up a cushion.

Write a list headed 'I am angry with ... because ...'
It takes a while to flow, but when it does – wow!
When complete, take it to your sink and make a
ceremony of burning it (safely).

Find a place where you can shout in privacy and let go
verbally. My exercise class used to encourage us to scream
at the beginning of the session. As a supporter of
Tottenham Hotspur I find that I can release my emotions
regularly by shouting at them! Most spectator sports,
theatre and live music events can help people. It's called
catharsis in textbooks, but to the majority of us it is
letting off steam.

And if you are fit and taking regular exercise (otherwise please check with your doctor):

Take part in an aerobic sport, to the point of perspiration;

beat up a squash ball; go for a long fast run; or
even clean the house from top to bottom.

These are all ways of releasing anger, letting it out safely. It is
not appropriate to let it out on your family or friends – after
all, it isn't anything to do with them. But remember that the
watchword is safety. Don't let yourself get involved in
anything that might harm you. I know people who have hit
walls in frustration and then ended up in casualty with
damaged hands and arms.

Some people have found that the emotions build up to such
an extent that they feel upset and are frequently on the verge
of tears. If you feel like this, let yourself go. Hire a good weepy
video (or read *Love Story* yet again) and wallow. Let it all out
appropriately; it is much better out than in.

Listen to your body. Check your emotions regularly. If you
want to sleep a lot, then do so, and eat sensibly and take
exercise as well. If you are feeling incredibly tired all the time
and you fight it, the chances are that you will become ill, as the
body has to have its own way in the end. So be nice to it and
make the first move.

If you are having trouble sleeping, listen to your worries and
see if there is anything positive that you can do to resolve them.
Cut out caffeine; have a bath before you go to bed; see if you
can find a night-time drink that works for you (camomile tea,
milk, etc); find yourself a good relaxation tape and use it
regularly. Health food shops sell gentle sleeping pills that are
not addictive. I tend to avoid going to see my doctor for
relaxants or sleeping pills because of their addictive nature,
but if you are really suffering, don't be a martyr. Sleep is
important and a good night's rest will help you enormously. I
also tend to avoid alcohol as a nightcap because it is a
depressant.

Massage and aromatherapy can be very relaxing. Try it and
give yourself a treat. It can induce refreshing sleep – it does for
me, and I still sleep well at night afterwards

Organise time with people who will understand. Being in
contact with people is very important. When we are depressed,

we often withdraw, which doesn't help. The exchange of communication, affection and understanding is wonderfully healing.

Children can be valuable in releasing you from the 'pit'. Playing with a child makes you realise that life isn't that complicated as children are gloriously simplistic in their outlook. They don't worry about the future. They live 'in the moment'. Are they hungry, tired, bored, having fun, being loved, being concentrated on? That's what's important. And we can learn a great deal from them. Hang on to how you are doing right now and try not to panic about what the next moment/hour/day will bring. After all, panic stops us from being able to deal effectively with the practicalities like money and work. So live in the moment and look to the future from a position of security. Then you can handle the next steps.

When the black cloud of fear and upset settles above you, take a large sheet of paper and write on it 'Things I don't have to do any more' and fill it in. The list might include:

> Getting up in the dark
> Commuting
> Getting dressed up each day
> Having to deal with X, Y and Z
> Covering up for other people
> Doing things I don't want to
> Doing things I don't enjoy
> Never having time for lunch/friends/exercise/myself
> Only being able to shop late night and Saturdays
> Working for other people

and celebrate them! This is probably the first time in your life that you've been free to live your life the way you want to. Enjoy it!

Now you can begin, very slowly, to work out how you want to live your life in the future.

Stress relief: strategies to help

We all need stress relief strategies, so here is a list to help:

Relaxation
Exercise
Laughter
Insight
Engage in relationships and communication
Fuel – what we eat and drink

Relaxation. Are you getting enough sleep? Do you wake up feeling refreshed? Try going to bed at a set time each night. What do you do that is truly relaxing? Relaxation isn't sitting in front of the TV with a drink. Take time out for some form of formal relaxation each day. Buy a relaxation tape and listen to it daily. Consider yoga or meditation which have proved to be very effective methods of relaxing and reducing stress levels.

Exercise. Both forms of exercise (aerobic and stamina building) are vital. It is important to release tension as well as build up the stamina to protect you from stress reactions in the future. Ask your doctor for a check-up and work out an exercise plan. Try to plan for 20 minutes of exercise that causes you to perspire at least twice a week. Swimming is excellent because it allows you to balance both types of exercise.

Laughter. This is wonderful. If you can laugh at yourself and the world, you dramatically reduce the danger of taking everything too seriously. There is a wonderful story about a man in New York who was in hospital, dying. He took control of his life, moved out of hospital into a hotel, hired a video player and mountains of Marx Brothers videos, and laughed until he was cured! If it worked for him, think what it can do for you. So have fun, find things that make you laugh until you fall off the sofa, and learn to laugh a little at yourself. You will be well on the road to recovery from stress.

Insight. Remember that all things pass – even losing your job. Life goes on. The world never stops – it just keeps rolling on.

All these uncomfortable feelings will pass. Tomorrow is a new day. Start a new life every day. And count your blessings. Right now this second, you are alive, you are well, you have family, friends, people who love you, you have food, a roof over your head. Don't panic about the future. Balance the long term with the right now.

Engage. Be in communication with the world. Tell the world the truth. Talk to listening friends. Be genuine in your relationships with your friends, family and partner. Give and receive affection. Make sure that you get lots of hugs when things are tough. Stress is very lonely so let down the drawbridge and let people in. Allow people to help you; share with them what you want from them. True communication is two-way – it involves talking and listening. So who could you support? You now have the time to contribute to others too. Giving to others often makes us feel even better than when we are receiving.

Fuel. What we put into our bodies has a direct bearing on how we respond to stress. Because the fight/flight reaction has such an effect on our digestion, it is important to eat balanced meals. Try to eat more fresh fruit and vegetables. Increase your fibre intake. Reduce red meats and fat. Caffeine should be dramatically reduced or cut out altogether, if possible, as it increases stress reaction. Remember that coffee, tea and cola drinks contain high levels of caffeine. Alcohol is a depressant, so limit how much you drink. Nicotine has a strange effect, partly helpful with a very unhelpful kick in the tail, so reduce or give up smoking.

Many of us 'comfort eat' when we are unhappy. The danger is that not only do we overload our digestion, we also end up fat – so keep an eye on what you are doing. Try a hug instead of a bar of chocolate. It really works.

In addition, do one small thing. Even a small step towards changing the way things seem can help. Have your hair cut.

Paint your sitting room. Throw out your old clothes. Whatever is really worrying you, consider one small thing that you could do to start changing it. If you are worried about money, sell something, talk to your bank manager, work out your financial position, etc. If you are worried about having nothing to do, volunteer for something. Take up an evening class and meet new people as well as gain a new skill. Consider retraining. Start networking. Read books on your area of work and expand your knowledge. Go and talk to a recruitment agency in your field. Buy your industry journal. Research other opportunities in different fields.

Stress relief: action plan

What are you going to do?
When are you going to do it?
How are you going to do it?
Help: who or what will help you?

Fill out your plan now.

	What	When	How	Help
Relaxation				
Exercise				
Laughter				
Insight				
Engage in relationships				
Fuel (food and drink)				
One small step				

Part 2

Life and Career Planning

5. What Sort of Life Do You Want?

This is the sort of question we have never had the freedom to ask ourselves, so it often takes a while to answer it successfully. There are lots of processes to help you: take time to work through them all. Each is likely to raise different aspects of what you might need in your life in order to be totally satisfied. And that is what we are looking for: total satisfaction.

Wouldn't it be wonderful to reach the end of your career (or life) at peace with everything that you've done and be able to say, 'I am satisfied; I really had a go at all the things I wanted to do'?

There is a real sadness about people who reach, say, middle age and continually talk about what they always wanted to do but never did because they feel it is too late to start. We have met a staggering number of people who say that they should have been an actor/pop star/parent/country-dweller/author, etc. What a shame that they never took a chance – it might have been exactly what they needed to be fulfilled. On the other hand, it might not have been what they really wanted, in which case, they would have had the experience of trying it, then letting it go of their own free will.

What we hope these processes will give you is some aspects

of life that you need to fulfil in order to be satisfied. And each of us has different priorities in our lives. So the first place to start is to work out what your priorities are. For example, where does your family fit into the whole picture? As Deborah (one of the inspirations for this book) discovered in 1986, she wasn't happy living a wonderfully successful life in Australia because her family were on the other side of the world. So she came back and rebuilt a great life here that satisfied all her requirements.

If you are in a relationship, consider carefully whether your career or your partner is the number one priority. It makes a difference to how you approach the future. It is possible that your partner might not fancy moving to equatorial regions to save the gorilla, and you might have to negotiate how to find the balance between all the aspects that lead to satisfaction. After all, it is possible to make a real contribution to saving the gorilla by not going to the rainforest. (Otherwise the gorillas would be swamped by people trying to save them!)

Whatever you discover for yourself, talk it through with the people who are important to you.

This is your life

Imagine that you are able to travel forward in time. You are now about 60 years old. You have arranged to meet a friend for lunch when suddenly a TV presenter and a film crew arrive and announce that they are whisking you off to a TV studio to record *This is Your Life* with you as the subject.

What would your partner, children, colleagues, clients, friends, acquaintances and neighbours say about you? What would you *want* them to say about you, your life and your achievements? Make a list in the box opposite:

I would like people to say about me ...

Often we find that our lives until now would only account for a sentence or two. It is the rest of our lives that contains the essence of what we want to be and do. Make the past the launching pad to the future.

Conditions of satisfaction

One of the reasons why we are often not completely satisfied with our lives is that the various elements aren't working together in harmony. Often, for example, our health and fitness don't support the energy and stamina required to do all the things we want. Our work may involve a lot of travelling away from home. We may feel that we don't have enough time for fulfilling relationships with our families. How often is our income sufficient to cover all our outgoings? How much fun do we have in our lives and in which category does it most often appear?

You need a large sheet of paper headed 'Conditions of satisfaction for my life in ten years' time'. Some headings are suggested below. Describe all the areas of your life in ten years' time, where you would want to be completely satisfied and have them all working in harmony and supporting each other. Look at the whole of your life, not just work and income.

Now start to dream. How would it be if you were completely satisfied?

Relationship (your loving partnership)
Health/Fitness
Home
Work
Money
Fun/Relaxation
Creativity
Friends
Family
Learning/Self-development
Philosophy/Spiritual development
Any other headings you need.

Be as specific as you can. For example, under home include its location, its size, what you can see out of the windows, what each room feels like, how many people live with you, etc.

In 1988 one of the authors worked with Linda Jane, a successful city broker, who had decided to move to Derbyshire in order to fulfil her husband's family commitments. She was unsure about what she would do and how she would cope. After half an hour curled up in a window seat with a pencil and a large sheet of paper with 'lifestyle' headings as above, she suddenly rushed back into the room and, eyes shining with excitement, announced that she was going to train as a furniture restorer. In 1992, she reported that she was living happily in the country, running a small business with a friend, preparing to start a family, attending evening classes in furniture restoration, breeding goats and dogs, and well on her way to being completely satisfied.

James, a sales director, created a full portrait of his life in the future which included being a self-employed consultant, a successful author, happily married with two children, and living in a beautiful rose-covered cottage in Kent. So far only a few small steps have been taken towards these goals but the fact that he has goals has made all the difference, as he now feels that he knows what he is aiming for.

The advantage of looking ten years into the future is that it is far enough removed to give you some freedom. You can create a life that is enormously different from today and have plenty of time to put it into practice. But that is the next chapter. These processes aim to create some possibilities about what you might do/how you might be.

These are creative processes. They involve letting go of logic and pre-judgements. It is important not to filter out what feels ridiculous. Let your mind flow; let it go where it wants to. Some of the more wild ideas often contain the grain of a brilliant possibility. Stay with it. Because you come up with outrageous ideas, it doesn't mean that you have to put them all into operation. There will be specific times in this book set aside for you to make choices about what you are going to do with your ideas. After all, you are the only person who can choose what the rest of your life will contain. This book is about giving you permission to have the life you've always wanted, even if you didn't know what it was.

When were you happiest, and why?

Describe the time in your life when you were most happy and the circumstances around it. It may well provide you with a clue about more conditions of satisfaction. Paul, a senior manager, was able to identify a job he had had some years previously where he was working in a team of highly committed people on a task that they all believed in, and where the atmosphere was relaxed and happy as well as highly productive. Looking at what had made that time so enjoyable, enabled him to set some new standards for his future. Make your list on the next page.

When were you happiest, and why?

What's missing?

When you were in your job, what was missing in your life? Be as specific as possible. If the answer 'friends' comes up, what sort of friends, how many, what would they be doing with you/for you? Now that you are not working, what is missing? The same advice stands. If you answer 'job' and 'money', be specific about them. How much money? What sort of job? Is it the task (what you do) or the process (how, conditions of work)? Many people find that they miss the interaction with colleagues as opposed to the actual job task. But it is possible to create an interaction with people without it being tied to a particular task. There are so many possibilities when you are designing your own life.

What is missing in your life?

In our experience of working on these processes, some answers can be conceptual and there is nothing wrong with that. John, a manager in the City, realised that he wanted to ensure that London remains the financial capital of Europe rather than just go for status and money. This gave him an edge at interviews because he was able to communicate his vision so powerfully. He now has a position that might lead to achieving his dream.

Somehow, making a list of what is 'missing' is a powerful way of getting in touch with what is not working for us. When we write the phrase or word that sums it up, a bell nearly always rings. Sometimes people write very long lists but, when you ask which is the crucial point, they nearly always know.

Creating the future

Now transfer the results from the exercises so far on to this sheet and check that they work together. The headings are repeated.

As at (date) ....

In order to be fulfilled my future will include the following:

What will people say about you?

Conditions of satisfaction

When were you happiest and why?

What's missing in your life?

The map of your future

Take your list from the previous page, copy it on to small pieces of paper or card, and start to create patterns that make sense to you. You've got a mass of information that contains the essence of what you need in your future in order to be completely satisfied. Now you need to make sure that they all work together. For example, will your work support the salary you want? Does living in the sort of house you describe match the salary? Are the locations of your work and home compatible?

Keep juggling it all like a jigsaw puzzle until it begins to make sense as a whole picture. You might find that there is one item that doesn't fit, in which case take it out and reconsider its importance. Keep reprioritising and balancing until it makes sense.

This can be a time-consuming process. Don't panic. It's important enough to need lots of time. If you begin to despair, leave it alone for a while and come back to it when you are fresh. Total satisfaction is too important to rush.

Planning

When the picture is complete and fits together nicely, you have your future on paper. Now you have to create a plan that enables you to get there. Sometimes this can look rather intimidating because there is such a gap between where you are now and where you want to be. What you need is a *plan*.

I love plans. I think of them as route maps. If I am at present in the equivalent of Southampton and I think of my future as Edinburgh, I certainly need some sort of route to help me find my way. There are so many alternative routes, I need to work out what is best for me. For example, am I a motorway person or a B road person? I find a plan useful for keeping myself on track, *but* only if I look at it. I pin mine up in the kitchen so that I see it all the time. You may find it more useful to keep it in your diary. Find a place to suit you.

Take one of the major items in your future and, since this is a book about what to do when you've lost your job, let's start with that one.

Work out what you want to be doing in your new career in, say, five years' time. Write a short paragraph describing it and then work backwards, like a list of the towns between Edinburgh and Southampton. These towns can be the equivalent of monthly, quarterly or six-monthly goals – whatever works for you.

For example, you want to be head teacher of the Sixth Form College in Cambridge in five years' time. What will you need to have done, studied, achieved, etc in year four in order to be the ideal candidate at the end of that year? Likewise, what do you need to have done in year three in order to be in the right position to do what you need to in year four? Plan all the steps back to the present, so that you create various projects for each year, beginning now.

When you've got your five-year plan worked back to the present, you can be clear about what projects you need to fulfil this year and you can plan them with the help of the next section.

Projects
Projects are all the little elements that go to make up a plan. Using the route analogy again, a project is each town on the route. Projects are important because they break the task down into small achievable tasks, and provide a sense of achievement along the route because you will regularly complete some of them. Sometimes in the five-year planning exercise we don't know the answer to what we need to have done in year four to get what we want in year five, in which case it is the finding-out that becomes the project.

A project needs to be clearly defined and it needs to be SMART:

Simple
Measurable
Achievable
Realistic
Timed

How often have you said that you are going to get, say, fitter and yet you don't achieve this? Do you know why? Because it isn't SMART. Yes, it is simple but it isn't measurable or timed and therefore has become unachievable and unrealistic. We need to say the equivalent of 'I am going to lose a stone in weight in six months' and then work out *how*. There are plenty of options: exercise class, slimming club, swimming regularly, changing diet, balance between nutrition and exercise, etc. Then we need to decide how we are going to support ourselves: will we join a slimming club, have a bet with a friend, put the whole family on the same regime, exercise rigorously every day?

Another useful set of questions to ask yourself is:

WHO are you going to talk to?
WHAT is the objective?
WHEN are you going to do it?
WHERE would be best?
HOW: what do you need to do and what help do you need?

A word of warning: every area of life in your conditions of satisfaction is capable of producing a whole sheaf of projects. But don't take on too many or you will simply collapse under the strain and not achieve anything. Prioritise again and choose to begin with only two projects (one for your career and one for the other aspects of your life) and see how you get on. If they go well, consider taking on another one, but slowly, slowly please.

Remember that projects have a habit of reproducing themselves. Say you have a project to find out what an accountant needs to do to become a company secretary, and you go to see someone who can give you the answer. It may be that he gives you two possible answers and raises a whole set of new questions. You may end up with four projects from one meeting that was set up to complete the previous project.

6. Self-portrait

What we are trying to achieve through these processes is a sense of who we are as opposed to what we have done. When we go to a party and another guest asks, 'Who are you?', we give our name and tell them what we do. We believe that our value as a human being lies in what we do and that is one of the reasons why we find being unemployed particularly uncomfortable. So we *do* all the time, to keep busy, to stop having to think, and to give a so-called sense of value to our lives.

How about an alternative strategy? How about finding out who we *are*, and then discovering through that what we might do that would give full expression to who we are. This is a whole new ball game.

Qualities

One way to start is to ask your friends about your positive qualities. And different friends will come up with different qualities because, after all, we are often different in different situations. Make a list about yourself.

And ask your family. Ask as many people as you can (this is the start of networking). Remember to explain why you are asking for this sort of feedback, and give people time to do it for you. There is nothing worse than asking for feedback and finding that your friends are unable to come up with anything wonderful to say about you. Remember how unused we are to doing this for each other and allow everybody plenty of time. So you might get a list like this:

Enthusiastic
Good listener
Full of fun and life
Creative
Good communicator
Sensitive
Motivator
Proactive
Self-motivated
Leader
'A starter'
List your own:

_____

_____

_____

Compare the responses. If you receive similar answers from different people, you can be pretty sure that you are getting accurate feedback on how you present yourself. Single responses are slightly different. It may be that you show a particular quality only occasionally and you may want to change and show more of that particular aspect to more people. Sometimes feedback can say more about the giver than the receiver. For example, a shy person will see another slightly less shy person as being confident. So take the other person's personality into account when you are doing this. It doesn't mean that he or she is wrong. It is up to you to interpret feedback and decided which qualities you want to express.

What do you like doing?

In your past working life, what has given you a buzz? What did you *enjoy* doing? I don't necessarily mean what other people think you did best, but what made *you* feel great, as if you were really contributing? Make a list. And include any hobbies that you enjoy, anything in your life that makes you feel good ...

If this is hard, try making a list of what you don't like doing. It helps to unlock the process. Sometimes it is easier to work out the negative first.

Often we become trapped in the skills that other people think we possess and this limits the jobs that we are offered. That's fine, but in my experience unless these skills tie in with what we enjoy doing, then we never feel good about them. We don't believe in them and we are unfulfilled in our work.

For example, in my work in the film and video industry, because I love interacting with people, I had a reputation for being able to sell anyone anything. There was a certain amount of truth in this because I did relate well to people and, as long as I believed that it was good for them, I did manage to secure some important, valuable contracts. But what was missing for me was the daily management of people, which was what I really enjoyed. Selling/marketing was just something I could do, but it wasn't what I wanted to do all the time. It took many hours of discussion with management to stop them moving me into full-time selling on several occasions.

So sort out for yourself *who* you *are*, rather than *what* you *do* well. It seems to be the key to happiness and fulfilment in our work which is, after all, the purpose of this book. Your list of what you love doing provides a real benchmark against which you can measure what different jobs offer you.

Achievements

Now look at all the things that you have achieved in your life. What would you be able to celebrate (this may not necessarily be what anyone else would say)? What exams have you passed? Have you brought up a family? Have you bought a house or flat? What difficult periods of your life have you come through with flying colours? What have been your achievements at work? What were promotions given for? Have you built a successful team? Have you done anything that looked as if it might be impossible? What were your relationships with clients, bosses, colleagues and subordinates like?

If you have got to this part of the book and are feeling fairly comfortable, it probably means that you are learning how to manage change – a highly sought-after ability in our ever-changing world.

My achievements are ...

Transferable skills

What universal skills did you develop in your last job? What skills did you develop when you were being educated, during your working life, your home and family life? What skills have you developed in your hobbies or outside interests that would be valuable to an employer? Do you have any certificates? Have you been on any helpful courses?

Include all skills such as communication (both talking and listening), studying, research, reliability, time management, staying cool in crises, good telephone manner, well organised, able to make a presentation, writing, art, driving, organising a campaign, cooking, looking after a family, doing your own tax, etc, as well as all the generally recognised work skills like computing, accounts, sales, etc.

My transferable skills are ...

Now put together the results of these lists and write a self-portrait. This is the beginning of the preparation of information for your CV and interviews.

	Qualities
	What do you like doing?
	Achievements
	Transferable skills

Part 3
Finding a Job

7. Getting the Job You Really Want

The first six chapters of this book deal with handling change – the change caused by losing your job. You've survived the crisis, handled the emotions, rebuilt your confidence and created options for the future.

How do you realise these options? How do you secure the future that you really want and that fully meets your conditions of satisfaction?

You market yourself. If you were selling a product or a service, you would create a plan to maximise every opportunity for a sale. The process of self-marketing is exactly the same but, in this case, the product is *you*. Your self-marketing plan will need to be made up of a number of elements that correspond to steps of the sales process:

Planning. This is the key to making things happen, whether it be managing your projects, achieving your objectives, creating an office at home, designing a database to record information or deciding what to do each day or week. Planning, and working on your plan, will ensure that you achieve all the things you set out to do.

Knowing yourself. A good sales person knows his or her product so well that they are able to make the most of the opportunities available, handle the unexpected and secure the sale. This is what you need to do now to secure the job you really want. So knowing yourself, both strengths and weaknesses, is vital to your future success. Having worked this far through the book, you should know yourself pretty well and have a clear idea of the job options that you want to pursue further.

Presenting yourself. Your CV is your brochure. It is usually the first point of contact with a potential employer. It is a vitally important document that decides whether you are selected for interview or not.

Targeting your market. Successful sales people clearly identify their target market and carefully research potential customers. It is exactly the same with self-marketing. You need to identify the business sectors in which you would like to work, the companies or organisations that interest you, and possible methods of contact.

Making contact. This is a vitally important part of the process. You should not rely on one method of approach. It might lead to success but it is likely to take longer than if you had employed a variety of methods, and invariably leads to less choice. Using different methods of approach increases your chances of securing the job you really want.

Securing the interview. This needs to be thought about carefully. As much effort needs to go into this as designing your CV. If you are writing, your letter needs to be interesting and powerful. It should clearly request an interview as well as supporting and complementing your application.

If you are telephoning, you need to prepare carefully what you want to say. Be ready to answer questions and handle different responses.

Practice will greatly improve your confidence and performance.

The interview, or meeting with one of the contacts in your network. How you handle this will make the difference between success and failure. Planning and preparation are essential.

Feedback and follow-up. You should be monitoring your performance and seeking opportunities for feedback at all times. If you do this conscientiously and consistently you will be able to improve your interview technique and greatly enhance your chances of success. It is also important to review each step and its outcome. From this you can plan your next move and never miss an opportunity. You need to be proactive rather than reactive.

Securing the offer or how to consolidate an employer's interest in you to a point where you can negotiate a deal. Only then can you compare the offer and accompanying package with your conditions of satisfaction to decide whether or not this is the job you want to accept.

The following chapters look in depth at each element of self-marketing so that you can develop your skills and understanding and be able to approach each job application with confidence. It is important to address each element of self-marketing thoroughly and not miss any. So, as a reminder, the elements we will be looking at are:

Planning
Knowing yourself
Creating the right impression
Creating opportunities
Making contact
Securing the interview
The interview
Feedback and follow-up
Negotiating the deal

We have also included a chapter (14) on setting up your own business (for those who may be considering this as an option) – what it involves, the risks, the rewards and how to plan for success.

8. Planning

Creating a routine

For most of us, work creates our routine. It determines when we get up in the morning and when we go home. Work, and its related travel and planning, represents a significant proportion of our waking hours. At least 50 per cent, and often more. So when you no longer have a job, there is a huge amount of time that you may find hard to fill.

One option is to do very little, other than watch TV or mope around feeling sorry for yourself. This happens to many unemployed people. One of the side-effects of being unemployed is a loss of self-esteem and personal confidence, and being inactive for long periods will do nothing to restore these vital life forces. The less you do, the less you achieve and the more worthless you feel.

There is, however, a positive alternative, one that will support you through this difficult period and greatly increase your chances of achieving the goals that you have set yourself. This is planning. Creating a routine, that takes your new circumstances into account and enables you to get things done. Make effective use of the one thing that money can't buy – time – to do things that you've not had time to do before, and rebuild your self-esteem and confidence, so enabling you to grasp the opportunities that not working creates for you.

Planning is a personal thing and you can best determine

what meets your needs. You may already have an effective planning system, one that worked well for you while you were employed and just needs to incorporate your new circumstances.

However, many of us don't have a planning system or, if we do, it is so closely linked to work that it dies with the job. So if, like me, you don't find planning a natural habit I hope that the methods detailed in this chapter will work for you, either as they stand or in a modified form to suit you.

Before we start, I'd like to make one important point about planning. It must not become a straitjacket. Planning can be very important in supporting you in achieving your goals, but if followed too rigidly it can become counter-productive. Planning is a framework around which your life happens and it should be flexible enough to incorporate the unexpected. For example, if you have a bad throat or a long-lost friend arrives on a day planned for telephoning contacts, the plan needs to change. Planning is there to support you, not to take over and control your life. It is a support mechanism that allows you to do the things you want and to be successful in whatever you choose to do. Planning should also include the pleasurable things in life. All too often our plans only cover work-related activities and this can often lead to fun and relaxation being squeezed out. So ensure that your plan is flexible and that it includes relaxing activities as well as those that are work-related.

Keep your planning process simple. If it is easy to maintain, you will be happy to keep it up to date and it will support you in achieving your goals. If it is too complex, it will quickly fall into disuse and provide no support at all.

Setting goals

Effective planning usually focuses on the goals you have set yourself, such as: job-search targets, how you relax, fitness, and so on. It is important that, while these goals stretch you and support your personal development, they should not be unrealistic. If you have just started running, it is unlikely that you will be able to run a marathon in six months' time. You need to find the balance between your goals being so easy that they lack that all-important sense of achievement and so unrealistic that they are unachievable and lead to feelings of frustration, disappointment and worthlessness.

Your personal goals should be reviewed and updated regularly. As your situation changes, it is likely that your personal goals will need to change too.

Networking is a powerful but often greatly under-used asset (see Figure 8.1). Many people who have been made redundant find that they are spending much more time on their own. As well as creating a routine for our lives, work also provides much of our social contact so being unemployed can lead to a feeling of abandonment. This is where the network of support

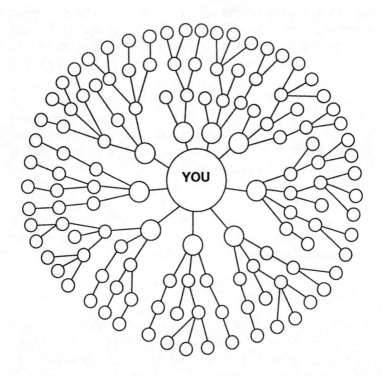

Figure 8.1 *The power of networking*

that you have created is of value. It allows you to maintain regular contact with friends or business colleagues who can support you in the changes taking place in your life. Your network is invaluable when developing and reviewing your personal goals and it can support you in drawing up and achieving your plans. You are surrounded by people who are willing to help you. Make full use of the support and expertise that they can give you. If they were in your situation you would probably be one of the first offering support. Reviewing your goals and plans with other people will provide an opportunity to be acknowledged for what you have achieved, which is important in rebuilding confidence and self-esteem. It will also provide a forum in which to review unachieved goals, and receive constructive coaching on the best course of action.

You can create a network of people who are in the same situation as yourself. They may be colleagues from work who have also been made redundant or people who live locally. You could meet regularly to share experiences and expertise as well as coach each other. This also provides a forum for creating ideas and developing new possibilities. Other people often notice attributes that you have not acknowledged to yourself, which could lead to new career options. This network could open up a new set of contacts.

If one of your career options is to be, for example, an airline pilot, it is unlikely that you know one through your own circle of friends. However, it is almost certain that through your network of friends, you will be able to make contact with a pilot who will be happy to talk to you about the job, and so allow you to gain an insider's view of what is involved. Use all your network contacts to their full potential.

Managing your projects

An effective planning process that works well for many people consists of only two items: a 'to do' list and a diary.

The 'to do' list
This enables you to keep track of all the activities you need to

complete. As they are all on one list, the chance of items being missed is low. The principle behind this approach is that your 'to do' list is a continuous process. New dated items are continuously added and then deleted when they are completed. When all the items on the sheet are complete, it can be destroyed. The big advantage of this approach is that you avoid the time-wasting activity of regularly rewriting and updating your list. You simply don't have to do it as the updating is automatic.

It is important that each entry is prioritised as it is entered. If you do not do this, you may find that you end up doing all the easy, less important things while the more difficult, more important ones are continually put off. Prioritising ensures that the important items are completed first and on time. You may find the following classifications useful:

A = very important; do immediately or as soon as possible
B = important; plan to do in the near future
C = less important; complete when time allows.

If any activities do not fall into the above categories they should not appear on your list. Figure 8.2 gives you an idea of what a continuous 'to do' list might look like.

Some people find it useful to prepare a daily checklist from the master list as it can provide a focus for the day's activities. However, it is an extra piece of paper and if you can work from your main 'to do' list on a daily basis, this is preferable. Do what works best for you but try to avoid having too much paper to manage.

From time to time you may find that you are faced with a difficult task or one that you are not looking forward to doing. There is a tendency to put this off, which is counter-productive. Often the difficult task is put off to the end of the day or even the next day. Sometimes we ignore it completely in the hope that it will go away. It rarely does and in the mean time it is hanging over us like a dark cloud. So if you are faced with an unpleasant task, make it the first thing you do that day. Then, instead of the dark cloud hanging over you all day, it is quickly out of the way allowing you to enjoy the rest of the

DATE	To Do	PRIORITY
15 Nov	Call - Graham re tax	B
	- Marilyn to state appointment	A
	Write to - Martin P - Unibox	A
	- Andy S - PSS	A
	- Roger S - Omag	A
	- Barry R - Constructors Ltd	B
16 Nov	Read Telegraph and Times jobs	A
	Swim	A
	Write letters to Plastics Plc and Unobank	A
	- Visit Library to research 20 more companies	A
	- Join local History society	C
	- Call John to return books	C
17 Nov	Go shopping	B
	Book Squash Court	C
	Follow up last week. Letters	A

Figure 8.2 *Continuous 'to do' list*

day. You may also find that your expectation is a lot worse than what actually happens. If necessary, do deals with yourself. Make conditions – you won't allow yourself a cup of coffee until the task is done or you will give yourself a reward when it is complete.

Your diary
This is the second powerful tool in your planning process. It allows you to allocate times to the various activities that you

are planning and, used regularly, it will ensure full and effective use of the time you have available.

Your diary should be used to plan all your activities, not just the ones that have fixed times attached to them; for example, a meeting, an appointment with the doctor, a tennis game, etc. Allocate time around the fixed items for the other activities on your 'to do' list and for your regular activities. Activities with no fixed time are things like researching potential employers, shopping, doing things at home, and making follow-up telephone calls. Plan these activities into your diary so that priorities are met and panic avoided. Figure 8.3 gives an example of what a week's plan might look like. It is much better to plan in your diary to research ten new potential employers a week, rather than leave it to the last minute and have to research 50 or 60 in one day. This type of activity can be draining if it takes up the whole day.

You may also find that breaking the day into units helps you to be more productive. It may be that morning and afternoon work well for you as units of the day, with lunch-time as a period of relaxation between two work periods. Some people find that they are wide-awake and active in the evenings while mornings are not a good time. If that is the case with you, you could do your reading, writing and planning in the evening. Have a plan that works for you. An example is shown opposite.

That is how simple planning can be and, if adopted, it will make sure that you do the things that need to be done. This will instill a sense of achievement leading to greater self-esteem and confidence. But remember, do not become a slave to your plan – build in flexibility to allow for the unexpected.

Making an office space

Making an office space at home is important. It becomes a focal point for everything related to your job search and a space where you go to work. It does not have to be a whole room and can just as easily be a desk or a table in the corner of your bedroom or sitting-room.

Creating this working space allows you to differentiate

Month JANUARY

Monday 12	Tuesday 13	Wednesday 14	Thursday 15	Friday 16	Saturday 17

Figure 8.3 Weekly plan

clearly between work and relaxation. When you are working this is done for you. You leave your house and go to the workplace associated with your job, while your home is associated with leisure activities and relaxation. It is important to have similar distinctions when you work and relax in the same place – your home. Your office at home will naturally become a focal point for all the activities and paper associated with work. It will help you if the phone is part of, or close to, this work area.

Managing the paper

Once you are working on your job search, it is amazing how much paper you generate and this needs to be kept in order. You will need to keep track of follow-up dates and make sure that your applications are in on time. Obviously, this links into both your diary and your 'to do' list. To keep track of and manage your papers, and use your time efficiently, you will find this filing system both simple and effective. It requires only five files, headed as follows:

Do today. As the title suggests, anything in this file has to be done today. Don't overload it and remember your priorities.

Do soon. This file contains all the other things that you plan to do not requiring immediate attention.

Awaiting information. Usually correspondence where you are waiting for a reply or where you've made a request for further information.

Read. Items that you plan to read that don't require immediate attention. You should plan time in your diary for reading so that the contents of this file do not grow to unmanageable proportions.

File. Items that you want to keep for future reference.

The Do today and Do soon files need to be checked and reviewed at the end of each day. If you do this, you will know that each day there will be no delay in deciding what to do,

COMPANY	PHONE	CONTACT	WROTE	FOLLOW UP
SUPER PLASTICS	0777 37112,	John Hopkins	11/11	17/11 Interview arranged 15/12
UM BOND PLC	0761 332211	Jane Brown	11/11	17/11 No interest at present.
MASSIMATOS	0777 444-333	Peter Smith	11/11	17/11 Call back mid December
GOLD SERVICE	071-666 4321	Mike Smith	14/11	17/11 Send copy of CV call wk 11/12
IRON Co LTD	081-977 3356	John Jenkins	16/11	23/11 Interview arranged 7/1
STAMP INC	071-333 2209	Elaine Almot	16/11	21/11 Not in call back wk 29/11
KENT LOTTERY	0277 519 42	Mike Jones	21/11	21/11 Will keep details on file.

Figure 8.4 Progress log

and you will quickly be in action. The other files need to be checked regularly so that everything in them is still relevant.

There is one more important heading that does not require a file. It is called Rubbish. Be ruthless with paper. If you no longer need it, throw it in the waste bin or, even better, recycle it.

You may also find a lever arch file useful to log your progress with target companies and advertised vacancies. In this way you can keep everything together, monitor progress and decide on the most appropriate follow-up activity and time. Figure 8.4 gives you an example of what this might look like. You may want to subdivide this file into headings such as: Network contacts, Agencies, Advertised vacancies and Direct approaches. You might even want to subdivide these further into the different industries in which you are interested; for example, security, retail, airlines. This file will link into your diary and your 'To do' list.

It is likely that, during this period of change, you will want to create a number of personal and work-related projects (see Chapter 6). If you do not have a way of managing these projects, you may soon find that important ones are being neglected and a disproportionate amount of time is being devoted to one at the expense of the others.

The secret is to manage all your projects concurrently. Carefully identify each one, be clear about the objective, the time-scale and the priority attached to it. Then manage your projects in line with your time-planning system to ensure that everything is completed on time and projects tackled in the right order.

Too often projects are tackled consecutively which leads to a stop/start process. It may be that you decide not to pursue a particular career option and, if you are not managing your projects concurrently, you will come to a halt, feel that you have got nowhere and have to start again. The diagram in Figure 8.5 clearly shows the advantage of managing your projects concurrently.

If you are working to keep financially stable but preparing

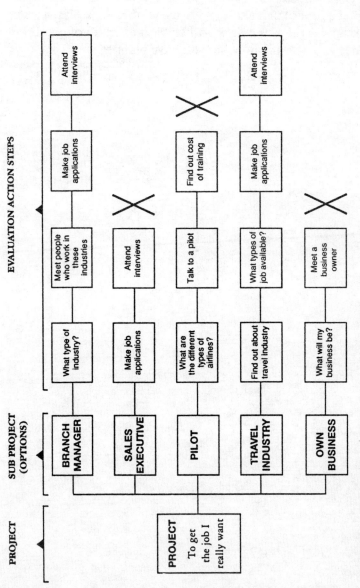

Figure 8.5 Managing projects concurrently

to make a career change, you may be wondering how you can fit it all in. Adapting the approach we have outlined will ensure that you can do it, although there may be less time available for you to pursue leisure activities.

As much attention needs to be given to the actions that achieve your plans as sitting down and planning. It is the doing that makes the planning worthwhile. A plan can only support you if you actually do what you have planned.

9. Creating the Right Impression

'You never get a second chance to make a first impression.' I am sure this statement is familiar to you. In achieving your goals and securing the job you really want, creating the right first impression is vital.

The right first impression is to present whatever you want to about yourself. This involves knowing yourself. Go back to Chapter 6, Self-portrait, which covers finding out who you are. Now comes the task of prioritising which aspects you most want to express to your potential employer and which are most relevant to the position you seek.

Your list will include aspects of you appropriate to creating a positive first impression and it is these that you need to identify. For example, a managerial position will probably require you to be a good motivator, a good communicator, a leader, an organiser, etc. So pull out all the appropriate aspects and prioritise them. Take the three that you feel are most important and use those as a benchmark for every communication. Throughout the rest of this book, bear your three main priorities in mind and concentrate on communicating them.

The first impression can be created in a number of ways depending on how you make your initial contact which could be a letter, a CV, how you sound on the telephone, or how you come across face to face (the most powerful impression).

Creating and building on a good first impression requires careful thought and planning. You may have a great CV but if you don't look the part when you meet the interviewer, that positive first impression may be undermined or, even worse, replaced by a negative one.

To raise your own awareness of how important first impressions are, try this simple exercise. For two weeks make a point of monitoring your own reactions to the first contact you have with people you don't know. When you meet them face to face, what assessments do you make? Are you categorising them into people who you would like to know better or not? It is likely that you are making this initial assessment, usually in one or two minutes, on physical characteristics which only represent one aspect of knowing that person. Also monitor how you react to letters that you receive and to the assessments you make about someone the first time you speak on the telephone.

If you analyse your reaction to that initial meeting, you will probably find that your first impression will feature strongly in how you continue to feel about that person. If you felt that there was something odd about him or her at your first contact, this feeling will probably always be with you. From this exercise you will appreciate the impact, both negative and positive, of the first impression and realise how important it is to create a good one.

Let's look at how you can create the right first impression each time you make a new contact. And remember that the *right* first impression is one that expresses *you* and whatever you want the potential employer to know about you.

Writing effective letters

Often a *letter* will be the first point of contact you have in the job-search process. Your letter needs to create an impact and be memorable. It should not be apologetic or contain negative statements, but should convey a clear, concise and powerful message. If you have been made redundant, or been fired, do not say so in the letter. The interview is the time to explain how and why you left your last job; you will then be able to observe the interviewer's reaction and overcome any concerns and correct any misunderstandings. If necessary, you can ask the interviewer how he or she feels about your leaving your previous employment.

As part of your job search, the primary objective in sending a letter is to secure a meeting to discuss a specific job or general job opportunities.

To write effective, powerful letters, we suggest that you follow these guidelines:

- Be clear about why you are writing the letter. Is it to request information, to secure a meeting or to follow up a previous contact?
- Don't rush your letter writing. Take time to plan and organise the content, and to make amendments before arriving at the final version.
- Use your support network to give you feedback.
- Design your letter to create impact and arouse the reader's interest.
- Do not include negative statements, jokes or apologies.
- Make sure that your letter contains a clear request for the reader to respond or an announcement of action on your part. If the latter, make sure that you do it.
- Always personalise your letter. Always send to a named contact (check the correct name and job title), never 'Dear Sir'.
- Avoid the temptation to send dozens of identical letters just to get a lot done – even the odd personal sentence or two can make all the difference to how it is received.
- Make sure that the message is appropriate to the reader and, if possible, include a comment referring to the company or industry.
- Use good quality A4 paper with matching envelope, preferably white. If you want to use a coloured paper, only use pale tints not bold, dark colours.
- If you can afford it, have your letterhead printed.
- Unless your handwriting is very good, type your letters.

If you are doing a big mailshot, it is certainly more practical to have your letters typed. If you have your own pc at home, or access to one, always use a good quality printer. It must be letter quality print.

- Ideally, your letter should be no more than one page – one and a half at the absolute maximum. If your letter is too long it is unlikely to be read.

- Pay attention to the layout. Make sure that there is lots of white space so that your letter looks appealing to the reader (who will then want to read it).

- Never use condensed type. Use normal type at 10 or 12 pitch.

Structure your letter as follows:

Your *opening* must arouse the reader's interest and make him want to read on.
The *main body* of the letter must only contain relevant information.
End with a clear request to the reader or statement of action on your part.

Figure 9.1 is an example of a letter to a network contact; Figure 9.2 is an example of a direct approach to a company; and Figure 9.3 offers an example of a letter to an agency.

Your CV

Your CV is your brochure, your opportunity to communicate your strengths, skills, experience and achievements in a way that will allow the reader to be clear about who you are and what you can do. It is the most important document that you will produce in your job search. With your letter, it is the information on which the recipient will make the decision whether or not to invite you for an interview. Remember that your CV is designed to get you the interview, *not* the job. (The purpose of the interview is to be offered the job.)

37 The Street
Newtown
Oxon RG13 3PU

Tel 0333 9687

26 June 1993

Dear John

It is some time since we have spoken. I think our paths last crossed about two years ago at the tennis club.

I'm writing to update you on my situation. As a result of a restructuring within Plexidom about two months ago I was made redundant. Although it was a shock at the time I have been able to take stock and now realise that a move was long overdue. Having the time available has enabled me to consider carefully a range of options that I want to look at further.

This is where I think you can help me. A couple of the options that I am exploring are related to your field of work and I would very much appreciate your views on my ideas. I'll call early next week in the hope that we can arrange a meeting.

I hope Joan and the children are well.

Yours

Jack White

Figure 9.1 *Example of a letter to a network contact*

15 Upper Street
Lower Hamp
Birmingham
B3 8AU

Tel 03 377 9021

14 May 1993

Mr D Johnson
Managing Director
Juno plc
Lexington Industrial Estate
Redland Lane
Oxboro CZ7 0TT

Dear Mr Johnson

I read with interest an article in the *Financial Times* last week announcing your company's intention to diversify and expand into the plastics market.

The success of a venture of this nature depends heavily on having the right staff in place at the right time with experience in the new field. My experience as Sales Director of Super Plastics plc has given me a broad grounding in all aspects of business and market development, communication, staffing and implementing change. I was responsible for a programme that increased sales by 10 per cent in a declining market and for establishing the sales and marketing strategy for a new division recently established by Super Plastics.

I enclose a copy of my CV and would welcome the opportunity of a meeting to discuss this further. I will phone you in the next few days to arrange a meeting, if this is appropriate.

Yours sincerely

Valerie Jones

Figure 9.2   *Letter for direct approach to potential employer*

14 The Hill
Hampton
Middlesex
TW77 9UG

Tel 801 466 7362

12 August 1993

Ms Jane Smith
Senior Consultant
Executive Search Ltd
Regency House
Regent Street
London W1A 5FF

Dear Ms Smith

I wish to further my career in the retail sector and am writing to you as I understand you specialise in this area.

As you can see from my CV my last position was Regional Manager responsible for 15 outlets. I believe I have skills and experience that may be of interest to your clients, in particular:

- strong leadership and management qualities;
- good communication skills and the ability to motivate staff;
- successful track record of increasing market share and introducing new lines;
- successful introduction and management of change.

My package was approximately £31,000 of which £24,000 was basic salary.

I would very much appreciate a meeting to discuss how my skills and expertise may meet the needs of your clients. I will phone you in the next few days to arrange a meeting, if you feel this is appropriate.

Yours sincerely

Peter Brown

Figure 9.3 *Letter to a recruitment consultancy*

The starting point for your CV is collecting data about yourself. In Chapter 6 you identified your life's achievements, wrote your life story and gained an insight into your skills, abilities and attributes from people who know you. This is all valuable information in developing an effective and powerful CV that will work for you by initiating the meetings that will lead to the job you really want.

YEAR	JOB	RESPONSIBILITIES	ACHIEVEMENTS
1992	REGIONAL DIRECTOR EXCEL	- General management Sales division. - 150 staff 25 branches - £18m turnover - Recruiting staff - Planning and running regional meetings - Preparing annual Business plan - Introducing TQM - Preparing monthly reports - Planning and implementing training for staff. - Selling to new and existing major accounts - Handling local press/radio	- maintained profit in recession - negotiated £1m contract with Oil Co - Reduced staff turnover from 128% to 47% - successful unit reduction BS5750 + TQM - Reduced staff without demotivating those remaining
1991	as above	as above	- negotiated £600k contract with Health Authority. - Introduced computers to improve admin and enable more time for selling
1990	as above	as above	
1989	DIVISIONAL DIRECTOR OF EXCEL	- Setting up new division - Recruiting and training staff - Developing new products	- Designed new training ahead of schedule - Introduced new monitoring systems.

Figure 9.4 *Creating a chronological career history*

You will also find it useful to create a chronological record of your career and education to date (Figure 9.4). Start from now and work back, year by year, to your last years in secondary school. Make this record as accurate, honest and detailed as your memory will allow. You will be the only one to see it, so it doesn't matter what you write – it can be destroyed when you've created your CV. The objective is for you to create an accurate inventory of your career.

Guidelines for writing an effective CV

Write it yourself. Your CV is designed to communicate who you are to the reader and by writing it yourself this will show through clearly. Use your network of contacts to give you feedback so that appropriate changes can be incorporated. Their reaction will also help you to judge how it will be received when making job applications. But remember that it is designed to advertise *you* so be careful not to change yourself out of all recognition. How you describe yourself at interview will then flow naturally from your CV. You will know the content intimately so there is no uncertainty in your mind about any aspect of it. If you do not have the facilities to produce a well-presented CV, have it done professionally but *write* it yourself.

If you have a CV that is two or three years out of date do not make the mistake of adding a piece to bring it up to date. It will not be an accurate statement of how you see your career today and could end up several pages too long. You will, no doubt, have had new insights into your achievements at work and these need to be included. A current, powerful CV will only come if you start from scratch each time.

Make your CV factual, accurate and honest. Most employers take up references, so any inaccuracies will be quickly spotted, which could mean a rejection letter rather than a job offer. If you have gaps in your career – for example, unemployment, maternity leave or a long period of illness – show them. Put yourself in the reader's shoes and anticipate what to include and how to make the biggest impact. Your aim is to have your CV in the 'Yes' pile.

Clearly list your achievements. The most common failing in writing a CV is the omission of achievements. It seems that communicating achievements causes the British embarrassment. We don't like to feel that we are 'showing off'. A list of responsibilities tells the reader nothing about how well you performed at work, and this style of CV is usually consigned to the 'No' pile. If you want the interview, detail your achievements clearly. Using action verbs (Figure 9.5) will give a positive feel to your CV and will aid the clear communication of your achievements.

Layout. There is no standard layout for a CV. This is one good reason for avoiding CV writers. They tend to produce to a specific layout and style which is often spotted by the interviewer and another reason why a CV may end up on the 'No' pile. Your CV is a personal document and the layout and style should reflect you and your needs. Guidelines for layout are as follows:

- Make it look good so that the recipient wants to read it. Ask your network for a readability rating when giving you feedback. You should be aiming for 10 out of 10, 9 is the absolute minimum.
- Make sure that you have a balanced presentation with sufficient white space to encourage reading.
- Don't make it any longer than two sides of A4. If you have a technical or professional background with technical qualifications or publications that need to be included, these should be on a separate sheet at the end of the CV (Figure 9.6).
- Use good quality paper. This will help it to stand out in the pile of CVs.
- Use normal size type. With today's word processors, it is possible to reduce the typesize significantly to a point where it becomes unattractive. Never try to cram everything in tiny type to make it fit two pages. This is a turn-off and your CV will end up in the 'No' pile.

accomplished
achieved
acquired
activated
adjusted
administered
analysed
applied
appraised
approved
arranged
assisted
attained
authorised

budgeted

catalogued
classified
coached
communicated
completed
compiled
conceived
conducted
consolidated
constructed
consulted
controlled
co-ordinated
counselled
created

decided
defined
delegated
delivered
demonstrated
designed
developed
diagnosed
directed
doubled

eliminated
empowered
encouraged
ended
established
estimated
examined
exceeded
executed
expanded
expedited
explained
extended

facilitated
finalised
finished
followed up
forecast
foresaw
formulated

generated
guided

headed
hired

implemented
improved
increased
influenced
initiated
innovated
instituted
instructed
interviewed
introduced
investigated

launched
learned
led
listened

maintained
managed
mediated
merged
monitored
motivated

negotiated

observed
operated
ordered
organised

participated
performed
persuaded
pioneered
planned
prepared
presented
processed
produced
projected
proposed
promoted

purchased

questioned

recognised
recommended
recruited
redesigned
reduced
released
renegotiated
reorganised
reported
researched
reviewed
revised

saved
scheduled
selected
serviced
set up
simplified
sold
solved
started
stimulated
streamlined
strengthened
stressed
stretched
structured
succeeded
summarised
superseded
supervised

taught
terminated
traded
trained
transferred
transformed
translated
trimmed
tripled
turned

uncovered
used

verified

widened
won
worked
wrote

Figure 9.5 *Action verbs*

- Staple your CV together but do not bind it. Binding adds nothing to the overall presentation and is irritating for the reader.

You may find that you need more than one CV. It is possible that in deciding what to do next, you are applying for all sorts of different jobs. One option might be a continuation of your career in advertising sales and another might be to get into the film or television industry on the production side. Here two CVs will be required. Each should emphasise the skills, attributes and achievements that will best support the different applications. Some examples are shown in Appendix 3.

The letter that you send with your CV is an opportunity to personalise your application with relevant information or comment.

If you are asked to fax a CV, do so then follow it up immediately with an original copy and a covering letter. Fax paper is of low quality, difficult to handle and invariably destroys the impact of your carefully thought-out presentation.

The content of your CV is particularly important. Applicants often include unnecessary information yet leave out vital facts to keep the length to two pages. Here are some guidelines on content:

- Personal details should be kept to a minimum. Name, address, phone number and date of birth. The first three are particularly important as your CV will often be detached from your covering letter.
- If you include a summary or personal profile, it should be the first item after your personal details.
- Your career summary should be in chronological order with your most recent job first. The amount of space taken by each job should be reduced as you go back in your career. The last ten years are the most important. Jobs you had 15-20 years ago need little explanation.
- Make sure that you include your main achievements.
- Include a chronological history of your education and

TECHNICAL EXPERTISE   Mary Smith

Word processing   DW1, DW4 (v1&2), DW5, DWA,
                        Textpack 2/6, Wordperfect v5.1,
                        Wordperfect for Windows, Word
                        for Windows (v2 & 2.0a), Typequick

Database   Rapidfile, Reportpack, 5520

DTP and graphics   Aldus Pagemaker v3.0, Harvard
                        Graphics all versions, PC
                        Paintbrush, Chartpack, Scangal

Conversion   PDQ, Software Bridge, Word for
                        Word, Word Doctor

Communications   Displaycomm, E Mail

Other   Virus Software, Norton Utilities, PC
                        Tools, MS Dos(v3.1 & 4.0),
                        Windows v3.1, OS/2 v1.3
                        (Presentation Manager), Novell

Hardware   System 6, Displaywriter, 5520,
                        various PCs, MC82, Wang OIS and
                        VIS, Racal Milgo Modem, Canon,
                        Brother and HP laserjet laser
                        printers, Brother and Newgen
                        postscript printers, HP colour
                        printer, HP Scanjet

Figure 9.6 Example of technical qualifications listing for
                CV

training experience. Unless you are a student seeking your first job, it is not necessary to list each O and A level. Their cumulative number is quite adequate. When listing training courses, only mention those that are significant and applicable. If you have worked for a reputable company, it will be assumed that you have attended courses relevant to your position.

- Listing interests is an optional extra and a matter of personal choice. If you list them, keep it short and accurate. Some applicants put down an unusual hobby, long since dropped, and are caught out when they meet an interviewer who challenges them with expert knowledge of the subject. If you cannot substantiate your hobbies, doubts may be raised about the validity of the rest of your CV. However, if you have a hobby that is directly relevant to the position you are applying for, include a reference to it in your covering letter.

- Do not include your salary on your CV. Later we will look at how to negotiate the best package and show that this should be done at the end of the selection process. If you are replying to an advertisement which asks for salary details, include them in your covering letter.

Your CV is a critical document. It will make the difference between getting an interview or not. Allow yourself plenty of time to write it and get as much constructive feedback as you can.

Managing your telephone image

You may have the chance to create a first impression on the telephone; or perhaps there is a telephone follow-up to a letter you have written. What you are seeking to do is enhance the positive impression you have already created, not detract from it. You can create a powerful image over the telephone, but take care that it isn't an incorrect one.

When you first meet someone with whom you have had regular telephone contact, how often are you surprised by their appearance or age? A voice on the telephone conveys, perhaps, an image of someone mature and large while the reality is that they are young and slim, or vice versa.

As with letters and your CV, planning and preparation is all-important in order to make a positive impact on the phone. If you follow these steps, the telephone will work for, not against, you.

- Plan what you want to say. If it helps, jot down notes to remind you of what you want to say. If you forget to mention something, it may not be possible to call back to rectify the omission.
- If the purpose of the call is to make a request, be positive about what it is and ask clearly and confidently. If you find it difficult to make requests, practise on your friends, making two requests a day. If they are spoken confidently, you'll be surprised how often you get a favourable response.
- Speak clearly, with confidence and at a normal pace – not too fast or too slow.
- Believe in yourself. If you don't, how can the person at the other end of the telephone line?
- Smile and be enthusiastic. Believe me, it will be communicated down the line, as will an apprehensive or dull tone. What you are phoning about is a serious matter – your future – but you are allowed to be enthusiastic and communicate how great you are. Practise with friends on the phone and get them to rate your enthusiasm and smile factors. You should be aiming for 10 out of 10. This is probably the most important aspect of using the phone, so become an expert and you will see a significant increase in appointments and successful phone calls.
- Cut out the background noises. Turn off the TV and radio, settle the children comfortably in another room. Background noise is not only distracting for you but also for the listener, and could create the wrong impression.

- If the person you are phoning has an unusual name and you are not sure how to pronounce it, ask the receptionist. When you address a person by his or her name it is very effective and creates a more personal relationship.
- When receiving an important telephone call, keep calm. Gather your thoughts and think carefully about what you want to say. If necessary, write notes and keep them near the phone. If the call comes at an inconvenient time or you need time to think, apologise and agree a time to return the call.
- Be prepared for the unexpected. You may be put through to the secretary to confirm an appointment and immediately transferred to the boss who starts asking questions. You may be following up a letter, and the recipient is interested and asks you to tell him about yourself or why you're suited to this job. When preparing for a call, anticipate all possible eventualities and plan how you will handle them.

Interviews

It is said that interviewers form 80 per cent of their opinion of you in the first four minutes of the interview, so it is important to dress and behave appropriately. If you are hoping to work for a young fashion magazine, a dark navy business suit will probably be inappropriate. Something more casual but smart is likely to fit in well. For a large law firm, the dark business suit will be correct, while casual dress will be out of place.

If you can afford it, visit an image consultant. They generally do one-to-one consultations and some may run less expensive group sessions. Men and women benefit equally from this service. You will find out which colours suit you best, the style of dress that projects the right image for all occasions, and the accessories to complement your outfits. If you can't afford that, go shopping and try on as many different styles and colours as you can. Take a friend who you can trust to be honest and, between you, you will get a good idea of what suits you and what doesn't.

The object at an interview is to appear one grade up from the job for which you are applying. If necessary, do some research on what people wear to work in that particular company. You can always visit the company in advance and stand outside the door at lunch-time to observe people and their clothes.

- Wear clothes that you feel comfortable in, that you feel good in and that boost your confidence. Never wear a brand new item; always wear it in at least once in advance, otherwise there is a real danger of the suit wearing you rather than the other way round. Make sure that your clothes are cleaned and pressed. Make sure that your shoes are clean, smart, reheeled if necessary and worn in if new.
- Don't take your shopping or a supermarket bag with you. Have a smart bag or briefcase for your papers and a book to read on the train.
- Hair should be clean and well groomed. Men should shave and women's make-up should be appropriate for a business meeting. Jangly jewellery should be left at home.

How you handle yourself in the first few minutes also has an impact on that all-important first impression.

- Manage your nerves. Be positive and confident. Speak clearly and assertively.
- Shake hands firmly.
- Maintain eye contact.
- Sit right back in the chair, your hands on your lap and both feet firmly on the floor.

Plan a strategy for making a good first impression. Take note of what your friends say. Implement your strategy and you will be over one of the major hurdles in getting the job you really want.

10. Creating Opportunities

You should now be ready to hit the market. You know what career options you are going for; you have rebuilt your personal confidence and self-esteem. You are confident on the telephone, you have drafted brilliant letters and you have prepared a great CV. The world is waiting for you, and all you have to do is make contact with the right people.

So what's the next step? One thing is for sure in the current, highly competitive market: you need to be in contact with as many people as possible, in as many ways as you can, and with a high level of tenacity and determination. This chapter is about creating as many opportunities as possible for discussing your career aspirations and nailing down potential job openings for investigation and evaluation.

There are several key ways of identifying these opportunities and possibilities:

Networking
Advertised vacancies
The Employment Service
Recruitment agencies
Direct approaches.

Networking

What is networking? We touched on it in relation to planning in Chapter 8. Broadly, it is a mechanism for providing support. Most people do not use, or at best make limited use of, their network of contacts. Two things seem to get in the way: our natural British reserve and our built-in emotional view that we have to cope on our own and not burden friends with our worries. Under-use of your network of contacts is probably one of the most limiting factors to personal growth and the realisation of your full potential. Do yourself a favour – unlock the potential of your network of contacts.

To demonstrate the power of networking, it is likely that you have available the expertise and support of 6¼ million people! How do we arrive at this figure? On average, each person knows at least 50 other people. Write down your own list. Include anyone who you are able to have a conversation with. Your list will probably exceed 50. It is likely that each of your 50 people knows another 50 – so just by talking to your friends you have access to 2500 people. Their friends will take this figure to 125,000, and their friends will take the figure to 6¼ million. An extremely powerful resource for you to use to your advantage! You won't want to speak to all of them, but among them will be people who can give you the information and support you need.

Another way of describing networking is that you can get through to anyone living on this planet who you need to speak to by making five calls, if only you know where to start. The power of networking is the personal introduction. Even the busiest people take calls with personal introductions so there are two important criteria to consider. First, who do you know who might possibly be able to put you in touch with someone who knows your 'target' and, second, what might be in it for him to speak to you. If you are the friend of a busy person, you will almost certainly not give away his telephone number without being clear that it is in his interests. Even VIPs are approachable if you can deliver something they want. It is a two-way process. Sometimes they are happy just to be able to help, particularly if they were helped in a similar way in their career. If you wanted to speak to Sir John Harvey-Jones, for example (don't we all?), you would need to research all the things he is involved in so that you could investigate any links with your network before considering what might be in it for him. If you had already read his books, you might have some clues; alternatively, that might be one of the questions you would want to explore in the chain leading to him. He is so busy that you would probably need to be able to offer him a benefit.

So, draw up a list of the people you know, with their interests and expertise. You might like to group them under the following headings:

Family
Friends
Work colleagues (past and present)
Customers and suppliers
Professional contacts
Competitor companies.

How do you use your network of contacts? First, you have to overcome this in-built sense of self-sufficiency and the emotional constraint that will only allow you to give support and not receive it. Practise making requests for support. Identify what support you want and from whom, and then ask for it. Ask directly in such a way that it is all right for your friends to say yes and also all right for them to say no. They may genuinely not be able to provide you with support at this moment, but will be happy to do so in the future. Try not to be manipulative with your requests for support. This approach will usually backfire on you as they are unlikely to be fulfilled.

It is also not a good idea to ask the direct question: 'Can you give me a job?' It is unlikely that the answer will be in the affirmative and having to say 'No' can be embarrassing. It may also stifle future opportunities for support. A good approach is to ask for help and guidance. Most people are flattered by such a request and are usually happy to spare you some time.

If they have a suitable opening or know of a vacancy elsewhere, they will discuss it with you.

What support can be provided through your network of contacts? Your close friends can provide emotional support at difficult times: the day you receive a batch of rejection letters, when you don't get the job you were short-listed for, or when you feel so low that you can't motivate yourself to do anything. By talking about how you feel, the emotional upset can be handled and you can refocus on achieving your goals.

It is also a good way of checking out ideas. You may have created an unusual career option and not know much about what is involved. Through your network it is likely that you can get in touch with someone who works in the field. If not, you might try to expand your network by researching the ideal person to talk to and contact him direct. You can arrange a meeting and find out more – the positive and the negative aspects. Sometimes we are attracted to a job by its perceived glamour and an insider's view can show us what it's really like.

You can use your network to gather information. Many aspects of the job-search process require research and you will find that much of what you need to know is already within your network. Your network contacts can provide you with contacts and identify job opportunities that can be followed up. If you are a member of a professional body, include it on your networking list. Networking is extremely powerful, *use it*!

Advertised vacancies

Advertised vacancies are, obviously, a good source of job opportunities. But the number of jobs advertised fluctuates relative to the state of the economy. In recessionary times there will be fewer jobs advertised and your application will need to be carefully thought out and well presented. In periods of economic growth, there will be many more advertisements and again care needs to be taken with your application to ensure that you are short-listed for the jobs that appeal to you.

When tackling the advertised jobs market, the first step is to identify the publications advertising the jobs that interest you. You will need to research in the following classifications:

- *National newspapers.* Refer to the list in Figure 10.1 to identify the paper and day most appropriate to the job you are seeking.
- *Regional and local.* These range from large circulation regional newspapers to the free sheets that drop through most of our letterboxes. Evaluate the advertised vacancies in each to see if regular reading is appropriate.
- *Trade publications.* There is an enormous number of these. You will probably know what they are for your own market. If you are looking for a career change, you may need to check with one of your network contacts to identify the relevant publications. It can be difficult and expensive to get on the circulation list, so try to arrange to borrow a copy as soon after publication as possible.
- *Professional bodies* sometimes advertise vacancies in their publications to members. Again check out what is appropriate.

To subscribe to all the relevant papers and publications is expensive. The reference section of your local library should have all the national newspapers as well as local and regional publications. Main libraries should also have a number of trade publications. Check with the librarian to see what is available.

Here are some guidelines for handling advertised vacancies:

- Read the publication carefully and identify the jobs that interest you. Job title, salary and location are good criteria to use for the first scan. This should allow you to highlight the interesting jobs where you have relevant skills and experience.
- Read each advertisement carefully and identify the key words and phrases. Some will apply to the job description and others to the person specification. Compare your conditions of satisfaction for work and

Sector	Monday	Tuesday	Wednesday	Thursday	Sunday
Accountancy	Evening Standard	Independent		Financial Times Times	
Catering and Hotels		Daily Express Evening Standard			
Computing	Independent		Evening Standard	Daily Telegraph Guardian Times	Sunday Times
Construction		Daily Express	Daily Mail Evening Standard	Daily Telegraph	
Creative/Media	Guardian	Evening Standard	Daily Express Daily Telegraph Independent Times	Daily Mail Evening Standard	Sunday Times
Education	Daily Telegraph Times	Guardian	Times Education	Independent	
Engineering	Independent	Daily Telegraph	Daily Mail Evening Standard	Daily Express Daily Telegraph Guardian Times	Sunday Times
Finance	Evening Standard	Daily Telegraph Independent	Daily Mail	Guardian Times	Sunday Times
General	Evening Standard	Evening Standard	Evening Standard Financial Times	Daily Express Daily Telegraph Evening Standard Guardian Independent Times	Independent Observer Sunday Telegraph Sunday Times
Legal		Times	Evening Standard		Sunday Times
Marketing and Sales	Guardian	Evening Standard	Daily Express Daily Telegraph Independent Times	Daily Mail Evening Standard	Sunday Times
Secretarial and Office	Evening Standard Guardian Times	Daily Mail Daily Express Evening Standard Independent	Evening Standard Times	Independent Times	

Figure 10.1 *National newspaper advertisements: where and when to find them*

decide if the match is close enough for you to want to pursue the job further.

- Now compare the key words and phrases with your own skills, attributes, experience and potential. If at least two-thirds match, apply for the job. If less than two-thirds match, the chances of being called for interview are low.
- If you don't match the educational requirements but can offer relevant experience, it is worth applying. If a professional qualification that you don't have is required, there is little point in applying.
- Don't be put off by age limits. Staff are often taken on even though they don't meet the specified age range requirement. If you are older, emphasise your maturity and experience. If you are younger, emphasise your energy, enthusiasm and ambition. (You don't *have* to put your age on your CV.)
- Respond within seven days using first class post. Follow the instructions in the advertisement. If you are asked to write for an application form, do it. You are wasting your time sending a CV and covering letter. If you are asked to quote your salary, do so in the covering letter.
- If a detailed response is required, one where you are asked to state why you are so suitable, you need to research the company and its products or services. Phone to see if a job description is available. This will enable you to structure your reply and highlight experience relevant to the information in the advertisement and your knowledge of the company.

Completing application forms

This can be tedious but needs to be done systematically and well, to ensure that you stand a good chance of being called to interview. Bear the following in mind:

- Companies use application forms to speed up the selection process and help them compare applications. Such forms (same format) may request information not usually included in a CV, eg health. If you write 'See CV' across the career history section, it is likely that your application will join the 'No' pile.

- Follow the instructions and complete all the sections. Carefully read the application form from start to finish. Take a copy of the blank form and complete it in draft on the photocopy before filling in the original. Errors and obvious amendments will detract from the information presented. The draft copy can be kept for future reference.

- Complete the form neatly. Avoid cheap ballpoint pens as they tend to blob. Use black ink if possible as it photocopies better. An illegible form will be discarded.

- Be positive and assertive in the words you use and highlight your strengths relevant to the position. Take every opportunity to prove that you are the right person for the job and let your enthusiasm show through. Use action words (see Figure 9.5, p. 99).

- Check that your answers are consistent with any other information you may have provided, and that you can support the statements when attending interview.

- If there is not enough space, use an additional sheet of paper clearly marked with your name, the job title, any reference number and the number/title of the question you are answering. Many application forms are badly designed and do not allow sufficient space for the answer.

- If there are any gaps in your career, handle them as we suggested when compiling your CV (Chapter 9).

- If you are asked for referees, check with the people concerned before submitting their names.

- Ask one of your network contacts to read and comment on your draft application before completing the original. It is also a good idea to ask someone to read the application for errors before it is sent off.

- You will only need to write a brief covering letter as all the information necessary is in the application form.

The Employment Service

There is now a wide range of state-funded support for the unemployed job-seeker. The services offered have become more customer-oriented in recent years with the Job-Seeker's Charter which was introduced in 1992 and clarifies the levels of service and support to be provided to unemployed people.

Many jobs are handled through Jobcentres, although it is rare for salaries to exceed £20,000. Through computerised systems, they are able to identify local vacancies. The advisers tend to specialise in the following areas: professional/executive, clerical/secretarial/general office jobs, catering/hotels, and manual/unskilled. Find out which adviser knows most about the work you want and ask to be told about appropriate vacancies. Jobcentres are now much more commercially aware and provide a greatly improved service to local employers who, as a result, now place more vacancies through them.

After 13 weeks' registered unemployment, you will be asked to meet a claimant adviser to check your back-to-work plan and discuss how best to find a job. He or she will want to see evidence that you are seeking work, so keep copies of job adverts to which you have replied, letters from potential employers and a record of your job applications. You may be able to attend a job-search seminar (two days of expert help in job-search techniques) and/or a job-review workshop (for people from professional, executive or administrative backgrounds who want help in looking more widely at career options).

After six months' unemployment we hope you will either be back at work or at least close to it. If not, as a long-term unemployed person you are entitled to additional support. This takes the form of:

Jobclubs. Designed to provide you with additional support and help in finding a job. As well as advice on job-search techniques, you will work with people in the same situation as yourself which can provide both moral and practical support.

You will have free use of stamps, newspapers, telephones, stationery and other resources. Your benefit will not be affected and your fares to the Jobclub will be paid.

Job interview guarantee. Provides additional help ranging from: a chance to try a new job for up to three weeks withut losing your entitlement to benefit if it does not work out; a place on a one-week job preparation course designed to help you succeed at an interview with a specific local employer. Whichever option you take up, you will be guaranteed an interview at the end of it.

A Restart Course. It will help you to decide on the kind of work you would like to do, give you advice on which jobs, training and other opportunities would suit you, and help you to plan how to get a job. Your fares to the course, which lasts five days, will be paid.

Recruitment agencies

Recruitment agencies can be a good source of job possibilities. However, they primarily work to meet the needs of their client companies as this is how they generate their fees. Most consultants who work for agencies earn a bonus for successful placements and therefore tend to be selective about the candidates with whom they are prepared to spend time. They only handle those applicants who they believe can be placed easily. Recruitment agencies fall into three main categories:

High street agencies. These tend to handle a wide range of jobs with salaries up to £20,000. They broadly specialise in sectors of the market, such as office, industrial, catering, etc. As well as the large well-known chains, there are small local agencies which can be equally effective. Choose the ones that meet your needs.

- *Executive search and selection agencies.* These focus on recruitment for permanent positions in the salary range £17,500 to approximately £70,000. There are agencies in this sector with offices throughout the country, but the tendency is for small groups of one to three offices. They tend to specialise by type of job, e g accountancy, management, sales, engineering, etc, or by industry sector, e g retail, petroleum, advertising, electronics, etc.

- *Headhunters*. They are retained by their clients to identify highly experienced people to fill a particular job. They seek to persuade someone to move from one company to another and tend to work mainly with currently employed people. Their assignments are usually in the £50,000 salary range and upwards.

How to get the best out of agencies

- Using agencies is a numbers game. You will need to make contact with a large number to identify those interested in you, those you are comfortable with and those offering a good service.
- Be selective and brief each agency carefully. Let them know your exact requirements for the type of job you want – salary, benefits, location, etc.
- Identify a consultant in the agency and maintain regular contact. He or she will be handling a lot of people, so regular contact should bring your CV to the top of the pile and increase the likelihood of your being offered an interview.
- Use the consultant to give you feedback on your career expectations and your CV.
- The agency may have a standard format for CVs to be sent to their clients. If this is the case, make sure that you see yours before it is sent out and make any changes necessary to ensure that the presentation is honest, positive and clearly shows your strengths. When you are offered an interview, ask the agency for as much information as possible. Who is the company? What can the agency tell you about its location, size and business, the package being offered? Can you have a copy of the job description? Who will you be meeting and what are

they like? It is in the agency's interest to do this as it will improve your chances of success and their chance of a fee.

To identify the agencies that may be able to help you, we have included a list of reference books in Appendix 2. You can also contact FRES (Federation of Recruitment and Employment Specialists) on 071-323 4300, which provide a list of agencies for specific areas of interest. Yellow Pages is the best place to find your local high street agencies.

If you want to make a career change, it is likely that agencies will be less interested in you. As they tend to specialise, they usually look for people with the relevant background and experience. So if you want to make a change, you will have to work harder with them. You need to point out that your transferable skills make you suitable for the position so that they can sell you to the client.

Agencies can also offer you temporary work in their areas of specialisation, from junior levels right through to very senior positions. It can be a good way of earning money while you are looking for the right permanent job. At the more senior levels, temporary work is referred to as interim management and there are a number of companies who specialise in this. They include the recruitment arms of many of the major accounting firms.

Direct approaches

The direct (or speculative) approach to companies can pay dividends. Many jobs are never advertised and are sourced through a number of avenues, including the direct approach. It may be that your letter arrives when a vacancy is being filled or your CV arouses sufficient interest for an initial meeting to be held to explore the possibilities. This type of approach tends to be less competitive when compared with advertised vacancies and applications via a recruitment agency. However, there may be no current opportunities and you may end up with a polite thank you letter. It is also a numbers game.

Even with detailed research, you will need to make a relatively large number of contacts to be successful. If you contact eight or ten companies, the chance of a positive response is low. If you contact 80 or 100 companies, your chances of success are much higher.

Success using this method is greatly increased if your campaign is well thought out and well targeted. Careful research and planning pay dividends. You need as much background information as possible on both the company and the sector in which it operates. This can be obtained from national and local newspapers, especially the financial sections, news and current affairs programmes on TV and radio, annual reports and house magazines (if you can get them), as well as trade journals and magazines. Your network of contacts can be a valuable source of information about specific companies and industry sectors.

Directories and reference books also provide specific company data. (See Appendix 2.) However, they tend to date quickly so you will need to validate each company and contact on the list. The quickest and easiest way to do this is to telephone the switchboard who will confirm the information or put you through to someone who can. It is rare for companies not to confirm contact names.

Direct approaches must always be to a named contact, not a 'Dear Sir' letter. Think carefully about who you want to contact. If you are looking for a senior position, the Managing Director is usually the right person. If you have computing expertise, write to the DP, IT or MIS Director. If the position you seek is of a more general nature, the Personnel Director/Manager is probably the best person. If possible, find out about him or her. If he or she is very senior, look in *Who's Who*. Alternatively, try your network contacts.

Your contact letter must be well written. It must be relevant, informative, not too long, to the point and arouse the reader's interest. (See Figures 9.1, 9.2 and 9.3.) You should normally enclose a copy of your CV. This type of letter should end with a request for a meeting. Make sure that you follow up when you said that you would. A letter that is not followed up will normally be consigned to the bin.

Each method of job search detailed above could secure the job you really want. Remember that you may be drawn to one particular method, or even feel strongly that one method is not for you. Design a campaign that uses all five methods. It will greatly increase your chance of success. Job search is a numbers game. The more contacts you make, the more meetings you will have; this will lead to more interviews that will secure you the job that closely matches the conditions of satisfaction for your life.

11. The Interview

The work you have done so far is starting to pay dividends and you are being invited to interviews. How do you handle this stage of the job search to ensure that you receive job offers? In 95 per cent of hirings an interview forms part of the selection process. So it is unlikely that you will be offered a job without having to attend an interview. This chapter takes a detailed look at the interview process and how it can work to your advantage.

The purpose of the interview

What is the purpose of the interview? It allows the interviewer, usually in a structured way, to evaluate your skills, experience, personality and suitability for the vacant position. It is also an opportunity to compare each applicant and their responses to a similar set of questions, and make a short-list or selection decision. This is when you will be selling yourself and letting the interviewer know why you are the right person for the job. It is also your opportunity to evaluate the company and the job being discussed. Many applicants miss this opportunity and end up accepting a job, based on the limited information they have gained, that turns out not to be right for them.

Types of interview

What types of interview might you encounter? Interviews can vary significantly from a short, informal type to a selection process that can last up to two days. What you encounter will depend largely on the job, the style of interview that the company decides to adopt and, to some extent, the personal style of the interviewer. The more usual types are:

- *Short initial interviews*. When an employer has a large number of applicants to consider, a short-list of 15–20 people may be drawn up and they will be asked to attend a short initial interview of up to 30 minutes. This will usually be informal and gives the interviewer the opportunity to meet the applicants, ask some questions and draw up a list of perhaps six to attend a more in-depth interview. At this type of interview, it is unlikely that you will be able to ask many questions. It will, however, provide you with valuable information for a subsequent interview.
- *Informal/Exploratory interviews*. Similar to the above or, more likely, the result of a speculative contact on your part. It gives the interviewer the opportunity to find out more about you so that a decision can be made on the most appropriate next step.
- *Formal first and second interviews*. The most common types of interview, usually held when a small number of applicants have been short-listed for a first interview or when a few applicants are invited back for second and subsequent interviews. Normally structured so that each applicant is evaluated against the same criteria. Recruitment companies will sometimes hold initial interviews on behalf of their client, so that a short-list can be drawn up. Just as important for you, only here you are persuading the consultant that you are the best person for the job. Also a good opportunity for you to fact-find about the employer.
- *Group interviews*. Occasionally, the interview process will start with formal or informal group meetings, which

is usually an opportunity for the employer to present the company and highlight the benefits of working for it. You should be able to ask questions and it is likely that you will have an opportunity for one-to-one discussions at the end. But bear in mind that you will be assessed during this process. This type of initial interview is usually followed by more formal one-to-one interviews at a later date.

- *Assessment centres/Testing.* Many of the larger companies use assessment centres as part of the recruitment process. These can last from half a day to three days. Between eight and twelve applicants attend a centre at any one time. You will be asked to complete a variety of exercises, including group activities, individual interviews, ability tests, a personality profile and various tasks designed to check your suitability for the job. It is a detailed and expensive process that shows that the organisation takes recruitment seriously. The process will give the interviewers a detailed profile of you to compare with the profile of the ideal candidate and subsequent interviews will depend on the outcome of the assessment centre. Each applicant should have some feedback on their profile which can be useful in the ongoing job-search process.

- *Panel or board interviews.* Some organisations, usually in the public sector, will ask you to attend an interview with a panel or board. Don't be intimidated – this is not usually the aim of this style of interview. Answer each question directly to the person who posed it.

- *Stress or pressure interviews.* Used much less now than they used to be. Most interviewers are trained to relax you so that you can present yourself as naturally as possible. Sometimes the stress interview may not reflect the company's style but rather the style of the individual interviewer. Don't be put off; don't panic, keep your head and answer each question in your normal manner. This type of interview may raise questions in your own mind about whether this is the type of company you really want to work for.

- *Telephone interviews.* Some companies employ short telephone interviews to decide which applicants to consider for a formal interview. It usually involves answering pre-set questions and you have the disadvantage of no visual feedback. If you are called at an inconvenient time, arrange for the interviewer to phone back at a more convenient time.

You may experience a variety of types of interview and sometimes they take place in the most unlikely places. We have heard of interviews in the back of taxis, on trains and planes on the way to meetings, in airport lounges, hotel lobbies, etc. Be prepared for the unexpected and adapt to it. But make personal safety your first priority.

From the interviewer's standpoint

The interviewer's aim is to develop a complete picture and form a balanced assessment of each applicant by observation and judgement. The interviewer will seek to establish and evaluate the following:

- Physical make-up – appearance, mannerisms, health, speech, etc.
- Work record, responsibilities, achievements and evidence of the claims being made and how these meet the requirements of the job.
- Personal values and interpersonal skills.
- An evaluation of potential to perform the specific job as well as future development.
- Education, training, intellect and any special aptitudes.
- Personal circumstances – married/single, children, able to relocate, travel extensively, etc.
- Interests.

A good interviewer will cover all these areas to build a

complete picture of each applicant so that an accurate comparison can be made.

What do you want from the interview?

The interview is a two-way process. It is an opportunity for you to evaluate the company, and your objectives should include the following:

- To present yourself effectively and in a way that clearly demonstrates that you are the ideal candidate.
- To ask questions about the company and the job.
- To find out more about the person you will be working for.
- To get a feel for the style, values and culture of the company.
- To establish the package being offered.

Ultimately, the interview should enable you to gather enough information to compare the job with your conditions of satisfaction so that you can make a decision as to whether or not to accept the offer.

The stages of the interview

You will need to consider carefully each of the following stages:

Preparation
The first five minutes
The core of the interview
Closing the interview.

Preparation

This is particularly important and probably the most critical part of the interview process. Time and effort spent in preparation will pay high dividends.

- Complete your research on the company, adding to the information you identified in Chapter 10. Obtain a job description, company literature and annual report, if possible. Find out as much as you can about the company's products or services. If the company has sites that are open to the public, eg retailers, banks, etc visit them and assess strengths and weaknesses. Who are the company's competitors and how do they compare?

- Find out the name, job title and responsibilities of the interviewer/s and as much other information as possible.
- Find out how to get to the interview and, if possible, check the route and timing. If you are going by car, check on the availability of local parking.
- If you are given the opportunity, choose the time of your interview. Choose the first or last spot depending on whether morning or afternoon is your best time.
- Find out how long the interview will last. If you have other appointments for that day, it is important to allow enough time for over-running.

Plan the interview itself

- Develop and practise a five-minute personal portrait. Early in an interview you may be invited to 'Tell me something about yourself'. This gives you an opportunity to present yourself positively and make a good impression on the interviewer, as well as giving a boost to your confidence. Make what you say relevant, briefly cover personal details such as family, education and interests, and then focus on work achievements and ambitions for the future.
- Identify questions that may be difficult for you to answer and practise your answers. The value of this exercise is that you will have created a structure to handle any difficult questions, including the ones you have not thought of. Figure 11.1 details some common interview questions.
- Prepare the questions you would like to ask. List them and refer to them during the course of the interview. It shows that you have taken time to prepare, even if all

1. Tell me about yourself.
2. Why are you considering leaving your current employer?
3. Why were you made redundant?
4. What have you been doing since you left your last employer?
5. How would you describe your working relationship with your boss?
6. What have been your major career achievements?
7. What have been your major achievements outside of work?
8. What are your strengths?
9. What are your weaknesses?
10. What have you got to offer us?
11. Why should we offer you the job?
12. How would you describe your management style?
13. How would you describe your leadership style?
14. How would your last boss/colleagues describe you?
15. What have you gained from your time with (your last employer)?
16. What are the qualities needed to be a good (position you have applied for, for example, accountant)?
17. What do you most enjoy at work?
18. What do you least enjoy at work?
19. Tell me about your leisure interests?
20. Where do you see yourself in five years' time?
21. Why do you want this job?
22. What is your minimum salary requirement?
23. If we offered you the job in which area would you feel least confident?
24. Are there any questions that you would like to ask me?

Figure 11.1 *Common interview questions*

your questions have been answered during the discussion.

- Update yourself on current trends and new developments in the industry. It is likely that there will be a question related to this. If not, you may be able to include this information in your own answers to demonstrate your knowledge of the industry.
- If you think a previous employer may give you a negative reference, check back and reach agreement on

what will be said. In this way, there will be no inconsistency and you will be able to handle this potential disaster during the interview.

- If you have a particular difficulty, eg a conviction or a handicap, prepare what you want to say and say it, (only if you want the job) towards the end of the interview. Make it as positive as you can. For example, 'I have epilepsy. My medication is working well and I have not had an attack for 18 months. But I wonder if you have any concerns that we should discuss.' Let the organisation know what might be involved. For example, what, if any, is the average time off you need per year or how should staff handle an attack?
- Arrange a practice interview, ideally with someone you don't know well. If possible, tape or video it so that you can analyse your performance and spot areas for improvement.
- Think carefully about what you want from the interview and, if necessary, make a list for reference.
- Look at all the information you have and assess what you have to offer.
- Decide how you can present yourself to best advantage. Why are you the ideal candidate? If you don't know, it will be almost impossible to sell yourself.
- Practise not making any negative statements about yourself.

On the day
On the day of the interview preparation is equally important.

- Decide what to wear the night before. Make sure that it is appropriate and that all your accessories match and are in keeping with a business image. (See Chapter 9.)
- Have all the items you need for the interview ready in your briefcase or bag.
- Get to bed early and have a good night's sleep.
- Arrive with time to spare. If you are too early, find somewhere to wait nearby.

- Adopt a positive attitude about yourself and the coming event. The interview starts before you enter the building.
- Report to reception at least five minutes before your interview time.
- Conduct yourself professionally in reception. There is often formal or informal feedback from reception to the interviewer. If it is appropriate you may be able to ask the receptionist general questions about the business.
- Go the lavatory just before the interview. Ask the receptionist where it is. You can check your appearance and see more of the building.
- Decline the offer of coffee or other refreshment. You might spill it and it might even lead to you wanting to go to the lavatory before the interview is over. This can be embarrassing and cause additional stress in what is already a stressful situation.
- If there is company information available in reception, read it. If you have time, refer to your own papers and check over your prepared information.

The first five minutes
This is probably the most critical part of the whole job-search process. As we said in Chapter 9, interviewers form 80 per cent of their opinion of you in the first four minutes of an interview. A poor first impression is hard to overcome during the interview.

- Maintain friendly eye contact but avoid an intense gaze.
- Relax, be confident, be yourself and be enthusiastic.
- Smile warmly from time to time. Avoid a fixed nervous grin.
- Be friendly, pleasant and businesslike. Avoid being over-familiar.
- Give a firm, positive handshake.
- Wait to be asked to sit down. If you are placed in an awkward position (for example, with the sun in your eyes) ask to move and do it immediately.
- Sit right back in the chair to gain maximum support for

your body, both feet firmly on the floor, hands in your lap. This is the most comfortable and reassuring position and will help to calm your nerves. Remember to breathe.

- Keep the pleasantries short. No long conversations about the weather, sport or your journey. It is not businesslike.
- Body language can be a real give-away and can communicate your inner feelings as effectively as words. Sit still and don't fidget. Be open in your expression and avoid sudden or violent body movements, especially with your hands. Use your hands to reinforce your message, but not too frequently or vigorously.
- Avoid 'ums' and 'ers'. They detract from your presentation and can be annoying to the interviewer.

The core of the interview

This is when the interviewer will make a detailed assessment of you and build on the initial impression. Be enthusiastic about yourself and let your personality and energy show through.

In all the coaching we do on improving interview techniques, this is the area that we have to spend most time on. It seems that as soon as we are in an interview, we think that we have to be solemn and serious all the time. We bury our energy, enthusiasm and personality. An interview *is* serious, but let your enthusiasm show through and it will do wonders for you. If this is all you learn you will be doing yourself a great favour.

- Be honest at all times. This does *not* mean telling the interviewer all the negative things about yourself, unless you are specifically asked about them. Many applicants talk themselves out of a job by answering questions that they have not been asked.
- Avoid negative statements about yourself. If an answer to a question means making a negative statement about

yourself, make it and quickly minimise it with a positive statement to counter the negative. For example, prepare a few acceptable weaknesses and what you are doing about them. So when the question about your weakness comes up, you can say, 'I am aware that my time management could improve so I have enrolled on a course next Saturday.'

- Assess your interviewer. What sort of person is he or she? What is the style of interviewing being used? How is he feeling? Do all you can to support him and provide him with all the information he needs. If you have an unpleasant interviewer, don't be turned off. Answer and continue the interview in the normal way.
- Allow the interviewer to manage the situation. But, if he or she monopolises the interview or asks a lot of closed questions which require only 'yes' or 'no' answers, take the initiative and make the points that you need to.
- Manage your time carefully. Don't be drawn into long irrelevant discussions. Make sure that you have time to get all your points across.
- Listen carefully to all the questions. If you don't understand or haven't heard the question, ask for clarification. Don't anticipate the end of questions – you may end up answering the wrong one.
- Don't ramble on. Keep your answers to the point and talk about your achievements. Substantiate any claims you make but be careful not to exaggerate.
- Don't be afraid of silences. They are always much shorter than you think. If you can't answer a question immediately, a short silence conveys thoughtfulness and maturity. Filling a silence with worthless words has the opposite effect.
- Make sure that you have an opportunity to ask your questions.
- Make regular assessments of the progress of the interview and take corrective action if necessary. In preparing for the interview, you will have identified all the important points that you want to communicate. If

this has not been achieved two-thirds of the way through, find a way of introducing those that have been missed.

- A good technique for reinforcing your positive points and ensuring your message comes across is to adopt the *Nine O'Clock News* technique. You start with the headlines, in your case the strong points relative to this job, report on them in detail during the interview, and summarise at the end.

Closing the interview

When the interview has come to an end, it is important to continue making a positive impression.

- Thank the interviewer for his or her time and, if appropriate, confirm your interest in the position.
- Ask what the next step will be.
- The interviewer may guide you back to reception and, in some buildings, this can take up to five minutes. Don't ruin your performance with casual, inappropriate comments. The interview has finished so make polite conversation on appropriate subjects.

The second interview

When you are invited for a second interview, your preparation needs to be just as careful and thorough. Here are some points to watch out for:

- Check who you will be meeting. If it's the same person as before there will be no need to cover background information. If you are meeting new people, find out their names and titles. Be prepared to present your personal portrait again and to cover any or all of the questions from the first interview.
- Prepare new questions that you would like to ask. You have more information now and will be expected to ask more detailed and probing questions.
- Don't relax *too* much. You may let yourself down.

- If you meet new people, get their views on the company and its values and culture and compare them with your first impressions.

What to beware of at interviews

- Don't attempt to negotiate the package until you are offered the job. When you have received a definite offer, you will be in a much stronger position and you should be able to negotiate a better deal.
- If you are asked about your previous salary, quote the total package value.
- Don't criticise former employers or colleagues.
- Beware of inaccurate statements as to why you left previous employers. If you were made redundant, say so. The stigma of redundancy has all but gone and few companies will hold this against you. If you were fired, say so. Keep the explanations brief.
- Don't smoke when invited to unless everyone else does. If you are a smoker, declare it but say that you had one before you arrived.
- Avoid talking about domestic or personal issues unless asked to do so, or if they are relevant to your application.
- Don't present material, such as references, exam certificates, samples of work, etc, unless asked to do so.
- Don't encroach on the interviewer's space. Don't lean on his or her desk or table. Don't move things on the desk or in the room.

After the interview

Reviewing your performance after an interview is as important as preparation before it. The sooner you can do this, the better, while everything is still fresh in your mind. Be honest with yourself. Ask yourself:

- Did I get everything across that I wanted to?

- How would I assess the outcome of the interview? Where did I not perform well and what can I do to improve in future? What went well that can be built on for future interviews?
- Do I feel that I presented the real me?
- How did I feel in the interview? If I felt nervous or tense, what caused this and how can I overcome it in the future?
- Did I establish a good rapport with the interviewer? If not, why not, and what can I do in the future to ensure that this does not happen again?
- Were there any difficult questions and how can I handle these well in the future?

If you feel it is appropriate, send a short letter confirming your interest in the position. If the interview came through an agency, check with the consultant for feedback.

If you are not asked to attend a second interview, take a deep breath and remember:

It does not mean that you are a failure.
It does not mean that you would not have done the job well.
It might mean simply that the company feels that you wouldn't have fitted in.

You might want to get feedback from the interviewer. If you decide to ask for this, act while the interview is still fresh in the interviewer's mind. This can be useful in improving future performance.

12. Negotiating the Deal

Your prospective employer will want to secure your services for the lowest reasonable package; your aim is to obtain the best possible deal. When you are offered a job, bear the following in mind.

Money is not a long-term motivator. It may meet your short-term basic needs, but if the job itself is not what you want you may find that you are soon disillusioned and keen to move on. If you do have to accept a job because you need the money, don't lose sight of your vision of how you want your life to be. See if, in some way, it can be achieved from what you are doing now. If not, continue your job search until you have the job that fully meets your conditions of satisfaction for life.

Consider what is being offered against your vision of how you want your life to be. Check each condition of satisfaction and see how closely they match. If any of your prime conditions have not been met, and cannot be negotiated to your satisfaction, the best course of action is to consider seriously if this is the right job for you.

Negotiate at the right time. When you know that the employer is committed to offering you the job, and that you are the preferred choice, it is time to start negotiating the deal.

Once the company is committed to you, it is more likely that your requests will be met. It is wise, at this stage, to check that the job *is* being offered to you. 'Can you confirm that you are offering me the job, subject to agreement of suitable terms?'

When the offer is made, maintain a short silence. It shows that you are giving the offer serious consideration and also suggests to the employer that perhaps the offer needs to be higher. Even if the offer appears totally satisfactory, do not accept immediately. Give yourself time to think about it. How does the offer compare with your conditions of satisfaction? What are your family's views? Are there any facts that you need to check out?

If you are expecting other offers that you want to consider, ask for more time. The recruitment process usually takes several months, so most employers will allow you a week or two to consider. You may also be able to use this latest offer to speed up responses from other potential employers. Whatever time commitments you make for declining or accepting an offer, keep them.

Consider the longer-term opportunities. What are the promotion prospects? What are the opportunities for personal development and training?

Do not under-sell yourself. Get a feel for the market rate for the job. Consider what you have to offer and formulate a package that you believe is fair. If the offer does not meet this, start negotiating. However, do not be unreasonable.

When considering your position, identify those parts of the package that, for you, are non-negotiable and those that you would be happy to be flexible about. If a base salary of £25,000 is important to you and the initial offer is lower, you may be able to trade off some of the less important items of the package to achieve this.

Clearly identify what you are able to offer the company to meet its goals and overcome its problems. You will have done this during the interview. Now you can restate how you can contribute to the achievement of a particular goal or how you can provide solutions to problems.

You will find that smaller companies tend to have more

flexibility in negotiating than larger ones, which are often tied to salary scales and benefits packages linked to seniority in the organisation.

You will probably want to consider the following:

- How much are you to be paid? Are there any bonus payments and how are they administered? What have the average, the maximum and the minimum payments been in recent months? Can you negotiate a guarantee for a period? If the salary does not meet your expectations, try to negotiate an early review, if possible, against agreed objectives.
- When are salary reviews and what is the policy? What have recent awards been?
- What is the job title? Who will you be reporting to and what will your responsibilities and level of authority be?
- What are the benefits – car, expenses, medical cover, pension, sickness benefit, holidays, notice periods, etc?
- If you are required to relocate, find out what assistance will be given. Also remember to get your family's views on such a move.
- What are the hours of work? What does the contract say? Are you expected to put in longer hours?

When you are negotiating, have confidence in yourself. You will have been through a careful and probably rigorous selection process and the employer has decided that you are the best person for the job. Negotiate a deal that fully meets your conditions of satisfaction.

Part 4
A New Start

13. Your New Job

Settling into your new job quickly and comfortably is very important. During the interview process you will have met at least one person or, at best, a small number of people from the organisation you are now joining. You have impressed them and they feel confident that you are the right person for the position. However, it is unlikely that you will have met the staff who will be working for you or many of your peer group.

All that we said about making the right first impression in Chapter 9 applies here. You will be meeting people for the first time who may be concerned about their new boss or colleague. They will be assessing you and drawing their own conclusions about what sort of person you are and how they are going to get on with you. How can you make the move into your new job as smooth as possible?

Before you start, gain as much information about your new employer, the market and your job as you can. You could ask the company to provide you with reference material before you join. You can research more in the reference library and add to the information gained at your interview. You can ask your network contacts for information and any insights into the company and the people you will be working with. Be as well prepared as possible with background knowledge.

You know more about the company now, so dress and behave appropriately. In your first few days, spend time listening and evaluating. If possible, arrange an opportunity to introduce yourself to your department. Keep it brief, smile genuinely, tell them how much you are looking forward to working with them, and ask for time to find your feet and for their help and support. Try to spend a little time with everyone over the first month. Don't jump to conclusions or put people into pigeon holes. While first impressions are powerful, they do not always stand the test of time, so give yourself time to get to know everybody.

Do not be too action-oriented. You may do something that you will regret later. Both your staff and your boss should give you breathing space to settle in.

Talk to your boss, your peers and staff about how they see things. What are the issues and the problems? What are the goals to be achieved? What do people think of you taking over? Was there an internal candidate for the position and how does he or she feel about you? Is there a consensus view?

Your first weeks with the organisation are unique. You have the opportunity to view the company as an outsider and you can take an unbiased look at what is going on. The longer you are with a company, the less you are able to do this. Make notes so that you can refer to them at a later date.

Spend as much time as possible with your boss. Be clear about what is expected of you. Confirm the job description and how he or she expects you both to work together. Identify the long- and short-term goals and how you will be expected to contribute to their achievement.

Understand the structure of the organisation and who does what. Identify the formal and informal lines of communication. Build a picture of the culture and values of the organisation. Do they fit what you have been told and seen in company literature? Get a feel for company politics and how the grapevine works.

Identify the key players and those with in-depth knowledge of the company and its products. They can be useful in increasing your knowledge and providing answers quickly when you are stuck.

Be friendly, diplomatic and enthusiastic. Establish your responsibilities and your level of authority. If in doubt, check with your boss. Be clear about induction training and how often you will meet your boss in the first few weeks. Identify your key tasks for the first few months and plan them into your schedule.

Most important, be yourself and live the vision that you have created for yourself. It is a new start and an opportunity to have things the way you want them. If you work long hours in the first few months to impress, this will be expected of you for ever after. Any attempt later on your part to reduce them may give rise to concern. Create a powerful first impression and one that you will be happy to live with while you are in the company.

14. Your Own Business

This chapter has been prepared as an introduction to starting your own business – one of your options for the future. Starting a business is the subject of many books in their own right (see Appendix 2), so if you decide that this is for you, you will need to do more research and take more advice than we can offer here. But there are some underlying principles involved which you can think about now.

The most important aspect of considering this option is to understand that cash-flow is king. Many small businesses fail, not because they are badly managed or unsuccessful, but because their cash requirements have not been sufficiently well thought through. We make this point now as it is important to the success of any venture and we will return to it in more detail later on in this chapter.

Is this a viable option for you?

The thought of having your own business can be exciting, especially if you have been made redundant and feel that the 'system' has let you down. You may also feel that you never want to be dependent for your livelihood on anyone else again and that running your own business will meet that need.

Remember though that, to some extent, you will be dependent – on your customers and probably your bank manager if you need finance or an overdraft facility. Balance the excitement and the desire for independence against the reality of running your own business.

You will need to think carefully about your own make-up:

- Are you the sort of person who is happy to take risks?
- Are you happy with the insecurity of not knowing how much, if anything, you will earn next week?'
- Are you comfortable without the security of a regular income?
- Are you happy to borrow money to finance this new venture and, possibly, put your house up as security?
- Do you need the support of a team around you or are you happy working on your own?
- Are you highly self-motivated and able to pick yourself up when the going gets tough?
- Do you consider yourself an entrepreneur?
- Are you good at selling? If not, do you have a potential partner in mind to sell you and your products/services?
- Have you often thought about setting up your own business?
- When the initial glamour fades, will you still want to keep going?
- Are you happy to chase people for the money they owe you?
- Do you have the support of your family and do they understand all the implications?

If you can honestly answer yes to all these questions, setting up your own business is an option that you can seriously consider.

Financial commitment

You must consider the financial risks and rewards of setting up your own business. You may have to invest a relatively large sum of money in starting up and be prepared to forfeit this if the business fails. You may not always be able to draw a salary yet still have to pay your household bills. Are you willing to put your house up as security for any loans you may need, and risk losing it if the venture fails? These are the negative aspects to the financial commitment you may have to make.

On the positive side, you are now fully in charge of your own finances. You will reap the rewards of your hard work. You are truly on performance-related pay. If you do not generate profitable income in your business, there will be no cash to pay yourself or the bills. Not all business owners end up being millionaires but many earn substantially more than they did when employed. There is also the opportunity for capital growth as well as income. A successful business can show a significant increase in value after ten to fifteen years, should you decide to sell.

Selling

The purpose of any business is to sell its products and services at a profit. It is not enough to have a wonderful idea, a good location, a hefty starting bank balance and a good management structure. A great many businesses fail because they are not supplying what customers want. Some fail because customers simply don't know what they are offering. Selling lives hand in hand with finance; without it a business cannot hope to survive. Any new business needs to bear sales and marketing in mind from the very beginning.

The different types of business

There are a number of different ways of operating a business which you need to consider:

Sole trader
Portfolio of activities
Partnership
Limited company.

Sole trader

As the name suggests, you are solely responsible for the business – its debts as well as its profits. Many freelance consultants, trainers, designers, home workers, sales people, etc, operate in this way. You may employ other members of staff or not. The benefits of this approach are flexibility, low overheads, simple administration and, quite often, easy entry into the market through existing contacts who provide you with work.

Portfolio of activities

This usually involves a sole trader who operates in a number of different fields, and it appeals to people who want variety in their lives. They may have discovered a number of equally interesting work options or take a lucrative part-time position to subsidise their chosen, less financially rewarding, activities. A typical portfolio might involve some consultancy work, a one-day-a-week job, lecturing at the local college, counselling and voluntary work. How your portfolio is made up will depend on your interests and financial requirements. Your portfolio can also be built around your own training needs and family or leisure activities. The additional benefit of this approach is that if one source of income dries up, you have two or three others to sustain you until this is replaced. This approach to work is a growing trend.

Partnership

This is where two or more people decide to work together in a partnership rather than a limited company. It is common in the professions and businesses that employ two or three people. There is the benefit of not having to comply with the requirements of the Companies Act, but problems could arise if you do not have a sound partnership agreement. For example, you may find yourself jointly responsible for another partner's debts, or your profits may be shared with the others even though you earned them in your spare time. Always consult a solicitor and ensure that a partnership agreement is drawn up, and do not sign it until you are satisfied with every aspect. If you do not have a partnership agreement, the provisions of the 1890 Act apply. A partnership is similar to a marriage, so be careful about who you become partners with. Much trust and good communication will be required to make it work. Consider all the implications and ask your solicitor to help you to draw up a check-list of standard items before you consider setting up a partnership.

Limited company

There is no minimum size for a limited company. A sole trader can choose to become a limited company. The benefit of limited company status is the limitation of some of your liabilities. However, in recent years the legislation has changed, making company directors much more responsible for the obligations of a failed company and the financial liabilities that result from poor day-to-day management. If you intend to be a director of a limited company, find out exactly what you will be responsible for. Another disadvantage for a small business is additional administration to comply with the Companies Act, and financial penalties for not doing so.

Figure 14.1 lists the main legal and financial differences between operating as a sole trader/partnership or limited company.

What will your business produce?

There are three main options to consider:

Buying a franchise to operate in an existing concept
Buying into a network marketing organisation
Creating your own business from scratch.

Buying a franchise

This is a way of having your own business in a tried and tested market with the full support and back-up of the franchisor. You should be able to operate as either a sole trader, a limited company or a partnership but check this with the franchisor.

Limited company	Sole trader/Partnership
1. Limited liability but you may have to give personal guarantees.	1. Unlimited liability for all debts, claims, etc.
2. Accounts must be filed within specified time for public inspection. £32 annual filing fee and late filing penalty (fine).	2. Accounts are confidential but must be prepared annually for the Inland Revenue. No annual filing fee or late filing penalty.
3. Accounts and full audit requirement. Additional cost.	3. No audit requirement or fee.
4. Class 1 National Insurance contributions for employer and employee.	4. Class 2 National Insurance Contributions with Class 4 on profits.
5. PAYE tax on directors' pay and effect this has on cash flow. Tax on dividends paid. Corporation tax paid on company's retained profit.	5. Tax payable on full profits but this can be deferred longer.
6. Details of expenses and benefits in kind have to be submitted to the Inland Revenue for all directors and employees earning over £8500 (P11Ds)	6. No requirement for P11Ds to be submitted each year.
7. Capital gains tax payable on the sale or winding up of the business.	7. No tax charged on winding up the business although there may be a balancing charge.
8. Shares in the company can be gifted	8. Difficult to make gifts for tax purposes.
9. Difficult to disincorporate and change to sole trader status.	9. If appropriate it is easy to incorporate as a limited company.
10. Company has to comply with Companies Act.	10. Companies Act does not apply.
11. Loss in first year cannot be carried back although it can be carried forward.	11. First year losses can be carried back to previous years.
12. Directors cannot borrow from the business.	12. Easier to transfer monies and to borrow from the business.
13. Pension scheme will be self-administered or executive pension scheme.	13. Pension provision will be through retirement annuity.
14. Possibly more credibility with other businesses and it may be easier to obtain credit.	14. In the early stages of the business possibly less commercial credibility and obtaining credit may be difficult.

Figure 14.1 *Deciding between sole trader/partnership and limited company*

The benefit of this approach is that you have a ready-made business that should generate income fairly quickly. The disadvantage is that you may initially require a large sum of money to invest in the business and you will be tied to the rules and regulations of the franchisor. The franchisor earns income in three ways. First, from the up-front fee that is levied to purchase the franchise, which can vary from £5000 to over 100,000. Second, from a regular franchise fee which is normally a percentage of monthly turnover. Third, from the sale of certain materials or products to the franchisee. Always deal with a reputable and well-established company. You will need to research how much potential expansion is left in the market; for example, there is a limit to how many print shops the market can support. The British Franchise Association provides valuable support and information. (See Appendix 1.)

Network marketing
This is also known as multi-level marketing and is relatively new to the UK. You run your own business within a network of similar small businesses which operate at different levels within the organisation. If you enter at the lowest level, you will be involved in the direct selling of the product or service and the investment required is usually small. You earn your income from the products you sell.

Moving to higher levels in the network is normally achieved by investing larger sums of money or by reaching predetermined levels of turnover. As you progress through the second, third, fourth and fifth levels of the network, you will need to attract more and more people into your own network. You increase your income by taking a percentage of their income and enhance your status as the size of your network grows. In higher levels of the network, you are primarily selling the business concept to other people who, you hope, will work through you. You will be asked to sign an agreement. Check this carefully and ask your solicitor to look at it as well. Check out the quality of the product that you are being asked to sell and ensure that any marketing claims can be substantiated.

The benefit of network marketing is being able to be in business quickly with back-up support from your next level networker. The disadvantages are often that the payment systems are complex and you may need to spend a large sum of money on products in order to enter at your chosen level. You can operate as a sole trader or a limited company. Like franchising, it is important to check saturation of the market. You will not be able to move up the network if you cannot recruit new members.

Creating your own business
The two stages of this process are, first, to think of ideas and second, to assess their viability.

It may be that you want to continue what you have been doing but work for yourself this time; for example, set up as a freelance accountant working for several small companies. You may want to use the skills you have acquired in full-time employment to start a business in a new field for example, a move from managing people in a large organisation to managing a shop.

Whatever you are considering, go back to the lists you made after reading Chapter 6. Think about what you like doing and what your personal qualities are and consider the possibilities. For example, if you are going to be dealing with members of the public, a love of people is important. If you are considering starting a business in a high-tech area, a degree of expertise (or at least access to it) is required.

But start with an open and positive frame of mind. What would give you real satisfaction? Look back at your conditions of satisfaction. What would help you to achieve them?

Why not try brainstorming? This can be done on your own or with potential business partners. The technique is simple. Start with a blank piece of paper and an open mind. The success of brainstorming comes from adopting an 'anything goes' attitude. Don't be inhibited. Aim for a hundred ideas in ten minutes. Say and write down whatever comes into your head. Sometimes the craziest ideas turn out to contain the seed of the best and most satisfying business ventures. Keep writing until you have an exhaustive list. Then consider each idea carefully and, where necessary, clarify your thoughts. Start to group the ideas together. There are likely to be one or two that are totally impractical but, before discarding them, consider whether they contain any useful 'seeds'. Discard all those which hold no real interest. Group the remaining ideas under broad business headings and see what options result. The idea is to narrow the list to two or three possibilities that you want to evaluate further. If there are more, that's fine, but your evaluation will take longer.

Now, find out as much as you can about each business option in order to assess its viability. It is important not to be carried away by the romance of the idea of running, say, a pub in the country, which is incredibly hard work and involves long working hours. Check the facts. Start with your library. Look at similar businesses – how they operate and what they charge. Do they look profitable? What range of products and services do they offer? Estimate how much money will be needed to launch the business. What are the working hours? What premises will be required? Could you start from home (check your lease/deeds and with the Council about business usage first)?

Use your network to get the inside stories. Find out what customers think. How competitive does the market look? Can you offer a better and/or cheaper service? Why might customers move to you? What would be special about your business? Is it a growing or declining market sector? Try to estimate the true market potential.

Collate all the information and prepare a short factual report on each business option. Discuss with your business colleagues or, if you are on your own, talk to contacts who can bring a business perspective to the discussion. Evaluate each business option. Decide which one is right for you and the market-place.

At this stage assess your commitment to your own business. By now you should be getting an idea of the investment required, the lead times in generating sales, how soon you can draw an income and how much this might be. Check again that you have the support and commitment of your family and the people who depend on you. If you do, this will make life a lot easier, particularly if things do not go as planned and you hit a difficult patch.

The next step is to develop your business concept. You need to be able to communicate the main purpose of your business easily and effectively, initially to the people you may want to involve in your business, your bank manager, etc, and ultimately to the people who will be buying your product or service. You should test the concept on as many people as possible. You will gain valuable feedback, become clearer yourself on the company's concept and aims, and gain practice in presenting your business concept well. You may find that it will go through a number of changes and refinements until it is right for you and easy for other people to understand.

You now need to test the concept with potential users of your service or buyers of your product. What do they think of your approach to this market? What would they be prepared to pay? Would they buy from you? What would make them change from an existing supplier? Who are your competitors? What is your competitive edge? Is it a growing or declining market? Can they offer any useful suggestions? Evaluate the reactions to this test marketing exercise and re-evaluate your commitment to starting this business.

Now do a detailed evaluation of your direct and indirect competitors. How do they operate? How different are they from you? How do they price? Is there an obvious niche in the market for you where there is little competition, or are you in direct competition? Through your network, try to arrange a visit to a similar business outside your area of trading. This can give you a useful insight into the business and some of the pitfalls to be avoided.

Make a final evaluation of all the information you have gathered and take a decision on whether to proceed or not.

Developing a business plan

If the outcome of the evaluation is positive, you need to

develop a business plan which will enable you to establish the financial requirements of the business and give you some idea of your likely earning potential in the first few years. What format the business plan takes depends on your need to raise finance. If you require a loan or finance from the bank, you need to prepare a detailed business plan. (Most banks have their own forms for submission, so check first.) If you do not need any external finance, your plan can be simple – just enough to confirm that you will generate sufficient income to pay your business and household bills.

If you are presenting a plan to the bank, it will probably need to cover the following:

- An introduction – an overview of the business proposal.
- Business proposal – the business concept, aims and objectives. An overview of the longer-term strategy and details of the tactical plan for establishing the business.
- Profile of key staff – half a page on each partner, director or any other key member of staff.
- Sales and marketing plan – a description of the business sector with both its short- and long-term outlook. A description of the product or service range. Your target market and competitors. Details of sales, marketing and promotional activities (including a monthly activity plan). Pricing policy and margins.
- Operating business procedures – details of how you intend to operate the business.
- A financial plan covering units to be sold, average price and margin, direct costs, fixed and variable costs, and profit and loss. Break these down monthly for the first year and quarterly for years 2 and 3. A capital expenditure forecast. A sensitivity analysis. (If sales are half those expected or costs double, what impact will this have on the business and the cash requirement?)
- A cash-flow forecast. This is the most important document you will produce as it is the best indicator of the viability of the business. To survive, you need to have a positive cash-flow as soon as possible. Remember

that unless yours is a cash business, you will probably have to wait 60 days for payment of your invoices. The cash-flow forecast will indicate your maximum cash requirement for the day-to-day running of the business. When added to capital expenditure, it will tell you how much cash is needed to start up. It will be one of the key factors in your bank's decision to lend you money.

- Finance requirement – a clear statement of your total funding requirements, how much you intend to invest and how much you want to borrow. Is your request for an overdraft, a longer-term loan or a combination of the two? Banks will normally advance on a like-for-like basis. The maximum they are likely to offer will match the amount you are putting in.

Professional advice

Always seek the advice of properly qualified professionals. It will be an initial expense but could save you a considerable amount later on.

- *Solicitor* – a great help with the legal aspects of setting up your business, whether it is a limited company or a partnership. Can give you advice on the wording of the various contracts you will need. Will help you to recover bad debts if necessary.
- *Accountant* – can be a great asset with financial and tax planning. A good sounding board for your financial projections. Will also allow you to focus on your business, while he takes care of the annual returns and the tax inspector.
- *Banker* – banks produce free, detailed and useful publications on setting up a new business. From time to time, some banks run promotional offers that will save you money. If you require finance, an exploratory meeting will help you to prepare your proposal in a way that meets the bank's needs.

- *Government support* – this changes regularly. To check what is currently available, ask your local Jobcentre and Training and Enterprise Council well as the Department of Trade and Industry.

Getting started

You have done all your research, evaluated the various options, tested the business plan and know that you have a viable business idea. You have also made the decision that having your own business is what you really want to do. You are ready to start. What do you do next?

Inland Revenue
Contact the tax office of your previous employer and explain what you are doing. They will tell you the office of your new Tax Inspector. If you have an accountant, pass the information on. If you are going to do your own accounts, contact the Tax Inspector and arrange a meeting. The Inland Revenue are extraordinarily helpful if you ask for advice.

National Insurance
Arrange to pay your basic stamp by direct debit to the DSS. The Inland Revenue will invoice you, together with income tax, for any additional amounts due.

VAT
Write to your local Customs and Excise office (address in the local phone book) explaining what you are doing. You will be sent the relevant VAT registration forms.

Raise the finance
You must be sure that the financial resources you need are in place before you start trading. Open a bank account for your business and deposit the money you plan to invest. If you have partners, get them to do the same. Arrange any loan and/or overdraft facilities that you need with your bank. Manage your cash carefully. Remember that cash flow is king. On

paper you may have a successful business, but if you don't have the cash in the bank to pay the bills, you won't survive for long. Devote sufficient time to keeping accurate books and to collecting the money that is owed to you.

At all times, make sure that you know the cash position of the business. In this way, you will know how much you have to spend, how you are performing against your plans and overdraft facilities, and how much you, personally, can take out of the business.

Get organised

Doing the right things at the right time will greatly enhance your chances of success. From your business plan, you know what you want to achieve in the first year. You can look in more detail at what you need to do in the first three months, and monthly and weekly and then daily. In this way, what you do each day will build towards your weekly, monthly, quarterly and annual goals.

Don't allow your planning to become too inflexible. Be able to move things around to take advantage of opportunities that come along and also cancel activities that no longer contribute to your longer-term goals.

Time planning is particularly important. Identify your priority activities and plan time slots for these each day. Identify those activities that need to be completed at specific times and plan them in.

Developing sales

This is the most important activity in any business, whether it be planning sales displays for a shop or telephoning potential customers. You need to ensure that there is always enough sales activity to bring in new business to replace contracts that have been fulfilled. Don't fall into the trap of easing up on sales activity when the first orders come in. You will be all right for a short time, but eventually your business will tail off as a result of the lower levels of sales activity.

Use your network of contacts to generate your initial sales. As they are people who you know, they are more likely to consider doing business with you than completely new contacts.

As we said at the beginning of this chapter, this is only a brief guide to some of the required steps. Refer to Appendix 2 for further reading.

Good luck, but, most of all, enjoy developing your own business.

15. The Ongoing Process

So you've got to the end of the book. We'll assume that you are now clear about what you are going to do and how you are going to do it. All done, finished, complete? Now, sit back and relax while it all happens? No, sorry. It rarely works out like that. Things happen, circumstances change, you change.

Once you have begun to take control of your life, it becomes an ongoing, never-ending process. You may have created a great ten-year vision and worked out a plan of how to get there, but it may be that a completely different opportunity comes up which makes you decide to go in a new direction, or you realise that what you were planning is not what you want now.

There are two important things to remember. First, you have a proven formula for clearing up uncertainties and clarifying where you are going. Second, any plans you have are *your* plans and you can change them without guilt whenever you need to. Plans were not intended to be written on tablets of stone. Plans are for revising as you go along.

For example, moving from where you are now towards satisfaction may feel like a journey from London to Glasgow. If you plan a route along the motorways, you may hit roadworks and decide that it would be better to travel on B roads to avoid hold-ups. Is that still following the plan? Yes. The route there may have changed slightly, but you are using your discretion about how to proceed in the most efficient way. The same applies if you are driving along a B road that looks as if it should be the perfect short-cut but suddenly ends in an open field. What do you do? Scream and shout? You may well do to get rid of your frustration. Sooner or later, though, you are going to have to turn round and go back and use a different route. This often happens in life.

It may be that, as you get closer to Glasgow (satisfaction), you realise that it isn't going to be good enough and the equivalent of Aberdeen is where you need to be aiming. There's nothing wrong with that. It is hard to recognise exactly what satisfaction means when we are a long way from it, so all we have is a picture of what we *think* it would look like. It is likely that we will need to adjust the picture of complete satisfaction as we get closer to it. This is why we need to create a structure and keep checking where we are.

As we said earlier, the world changes, circumstances change, we change our minds so it is important to take time to review where we are going. We suggest that you review progress every three months, but find out for yourself what is right for you. To start with, whenever life feels like it is drifting off course or you aren't feeling comfortable, check what you said you wanted and what you are doing about it.

Remember the headings for conditions of satisfaction. Write them down again.

Relationship
Health/Fitness
Home
Work
Money
Fun/Relaxation
Creativity
Friends
Family
Learning/Self-development

Philosophy
Others

How do you feel today, on a scale of one to ten, about your conditions of satisfaction. Check where you are now against where you thought you wanted to be. Check all your plans and projects. Are they working?

It may be that you no longer want what you thought you did, in which case you can start the process again in the confidence and relief that you have discovered another area that you don't want. This is definitely a plus, not a minus in the pursuit of complete satisfaction.

It may be that you are scared (and don't we all feel overwhelmed sometimes by the enormity of what we have decided to take on?) in which case the admission of fear may be a release, enabling action. The question is: does the fear outweigh the excitement that the original idea gave you? We all have days when nothing appeals to us and that is when commitment (and support from friends) comes in. Are you committed to being satisfied and are you prepared to work through this negative time? Our experience is that when we work through things and push ourselves into action, the negativity usually lifts quickly. And if it doesn't, it is often because we are working at something which isn't really what we want, so we need to start the process again.

But whatever happens, try to make sure that you sit down and review your progress regularly. Make a list of what you've achieved and tick it off against your plans and projects (this is a cheering exercise!). Look at what's working well and what isn't going so well, and whether there are any different routes you might need to explore.

Find yourself a coach you trust and share your plans and projects. By speaking plans out loud, you will be more likely to achieve them and by declaring your successes, they will become more real. Also, when things are not going well, you can call on your coach who can help you by asking questions. Because he or she knows how all your projects fit together and what the bigger vision for your life is, a coach can help you check through difficulties to see where the blocks are. He or she can help you to look at difficulties from different points of view so that you can assess them clearly.

Now here is the key to the whole book. *It takes an effort to be happy, fulfilled and satisfied.*

So much of our lives is tied up with excuses for not being happy: the wrong job, the wrong boss, the wrong partner, the wrong weight, the wrong gender, etc. The key to being satisfied is taking responsibility for our lives. No more excuses! The only reason why you may not be fulfilled is that you are choosing to let the excuses stop you from having all the things that you say are important to you. This book is really about taking responsibility for your life and choosing the right boss, organisation, people, location and salary. Our message is that you can have it all, whenever you want it. Just take charge of your life and decide for yourself what you need to be fulfilled.

So, remember:

- Review regularly your conditions of satisfaction and progress so far.
- Discovering something that you don't want is a success not a failure.
- Find a coach to help you be more objective.
- Develop your commitment to complete satisfaction.

Failure isn't when you fall down.
Failure exists only if you don't get up again.

Appendix 1
Useful Addresses

Alliance of Small Firms and Self Employed People, 33 The Green, Calne, Wiltshire SN11 8DJ; telephone: 0249 817003

Association of British Chambers of Commerce, 9 Tufton Street, London SW1P 3QB; telephone: 071–222 1555

British Franchise Association, Franchise Chambers, Thames View, Newtown Road, Henley on Thames, Oxon RG9 1HG; telephone 0491 578049

FRES (Federation of Recruitment and Employment Specialists), 36–38 Mortimer Street, London W1N 7CB; telephone: 071–323 4300

Institute of Directors, 116 Pall Mall, London SW1Y 5ED; telephone: 071–839 1233

Institute of Small Businesses, 14 Willow Street, London EC2A 4BH; telephone : 071–638 4939

National Federation of Self-Employed and Small Businesses,

32 St Annes Road West, Lytham St Annes, Lancs FY8 1NY; telephone: 0253 720911

Appendix 2
Further Reading

Self-development and awareness

Assert Yourself, Robert Sharpe, Kogan Page, 1989
Feel the Fear and Do it Anyway, Susan Jeffers, Arrow, 1987
How to Develop a Positive Attitude, Elwood N Chapman,
Kogan Page, 1988
Love is Letting Go of Fear, Gerald G Jampolsky, Bantam,
1982
Revolution From Within: a Book of Self-esteem, Gloria
Steinem, Corgi, 1993
The Road Less Travelled, Dr M Scott Peck, Arrow, 1990
Siddarthe, Herman Hesse, Picador, 1988
Vision in Action, C Shaefer and T Voors, Hawthorn, 1986

Health and fitness

Fit for Life, Harvey and Marilyn Diamond, Bantam, 1987

Business and employment

The Age of Unreason, Charles Handy, Arrow, 1991

Changing Course, Sue Dyson and Stephen Hoare, Sheldon, 1990

Creative Thinking and Brainstorming, J Geoffrey Rawlinson, Wildwood House, 1986

Finding the Right Job, Anne Segall with William Grierson, BBC, 1991

Getting There: Job Hunting for Women, Margaret Wallis, Kogan Page, Second edition, 1990

Getting the Right Job, Judy Skeats, Ward Lock, 1987

Great Answers to Tough Interview Questions, Martin John Yate, Kogan Page, Third edition, 1992

Manage Your Own Career, Ben Ball, Kogan Page, 1989

Setting Your Sights, Chris Brightwell, Ikon, 1991

Starting your own business

101 Ways to Start Your Own Business, Christine Ingham, Kogan Page, 1992

The A-Z of Self Employment, Sydney Bloch, Ashford, Buchan and Enright, 1991

Being the Boss, Stephen Fitz-Simon, Sheldon, 1987

Going Freelance, Geoffrey Golzen, Kogan Page, Third edition, 1991

How to Start a Business from Home, Graham Jones, How to Books, 1991

Start and Run a Profitable Consulting Business, Douglas A Gray, Kogan Page, 1989

Starting a Business on a Shoestring, Chris Dunn and Michael Syrett, Penguin, 1988

Starting a Small Business, Alan and Deborah Fowler, Sphere, 1990

Starting Your Own Business, Consumers' Association and Hodder & Stoughton, 1992

Which Business?, Stephen Halliday, Kogan Page, Second edition, 1990

Reference books

The CEPAC *Recruitment Guide*

The Executive Grapevine, Robert Baird (both give information on recruitment and selection agencies)

Kompass (lists companies by geographical areas)

Occupations, Careers and Occupational Information Centre, (classifies occupations and the jobs within them)

The Personnel Manager's Yearbook, AP Information Services (lists approximately 2000 major UK companies and contacts)

The Times 1000 compiled by Extel Finance (a list of the top 1000 British companies and information about them)

Appendix 3
Specimen CVs

Allison White
The White House, 37 River Lane, Highbanks, Bucks HP17 7SS
Tel: 0101 774432 (home)   DOB: 12.08.54.

PROFILE SUMMARY

Business Manager with broad commercial experience in IT and Service sectors with particular strengths in staff management, sales training, management development and practical formulation and implementation of Human Resources strategies.

CAREER SUMMARY

Jan 88 - Dec 92   **EXCEL SERVICES PLC**

May 89 - Dec 92   **Regional Director - Central London**

Responsible for general management of sales division of 150 staff in 25 branches, providing recruitment services to business. Reports to Group MD. Achievements:

- Generated sales turnover of £18m and maintained regional profitability despite recession.
- Successfully negotiated major contracts at senior level eg £1m with major oil company.
- Introduced effective new sales and management training which was then adopted at corporate level.
- Made significant improvements to regional Human Resources policy, reducing staff turnover from 128% to 47%.
- Created cultural change from autocracy to staff empowerment, improving employee commitment, motivation, and team spirit.
- Managed quality of service to clients and candidates in line with major TQM initiative and BS5750

Jan 88 - May 89   **Divisional Director - Office Technology Training**

Greenfield opportunity to set up new training division of 40 staff in 8 centres. Provision of end-user software training for clients and candidates. Sales and management training for staff. Achievements:

- Gained acceptance and credibility of division within six months by providing high quality training and service.
- Designed and implemented training strategy to meet corporate business objectives.

- Updated and expanded range of courses in line with market trends and results of training needs analysis.
- Increased public awareness by press events, radio interviews, seminars and presentations.

Jul 84 - Dec 87   MAJOR COMPANY PLC

**Oct 85 - Dec 87   Training Manager - IT Sales and
                           Marketing Division**

Promoted to head of department. Responsible for all training by division covering sales and management training and customer training.

- Managed 6 Training Consultants specialising in sales and management training, and secretarial staff.
- Selected, briefed and monitored external training providers.
- Reduced expenditure on external consultants by improving in-house capabilities in management training and development

Jul 84 - Oct 85   Training Consultant

Provided sales and management training for staff and developed courses for clients.

- Brought commercial skills to company moving from state-ownership to competitive environment.
- Conducted training needs analysis, designed and delivered courses. Trained trainers.
- Introduced new management training modules eg. leadership, performance management and assertiveness.

Aug 78 - Jun 84   BUSINESS SYSTEMS PLC

Aug 81 - June 84   Sales Training Officer

Promoted to Sales Training Department providing formal sales and management training.

- Presented management training courses and designed tailored programmes for individuals.
- Recruited and trained some of the most successful sales staff in the company.
- Regularly achieved top evaluation scores on training feedback.

Aug 78 - Aug 81   District Sales Representative

Responsible for sales of PC based business systems to commerce.

- Sold to decision makers at senior level (MD,FD,CoSec).
- Provided post sales training to customers' staff.
- Regularly exceeded 6 month targets for gaining new business.

EDUCATION

1961-74 NEWTON HIGH SCHOOL - 9 "O" Levels 3 "A" Levels
1974-77 UNIVERSITY COLLEGE - Psychology BA Hons (2/1)
1977-78 Post-Graduate Certificate in Education (Distinction)
Languages spoken/written: French, Italian

John J Jones
78 Hill Street, Brookpark, Cumbria CC3 8TS
Phone: 0044 15240

DOB: 19.02.62   Married

PROFILE

Sales, marketing and trading professional with a highly successful track record who consistently achieves tough but realistic goals. Proven ability to communicate effectively at all levels, developing and maintaining long term supplier and client relationships. Excellent negotiator with well developed team building and leadership skills based upon participative management style.

FUNCTIONAL SKILLS

- **Business Acumen**
  Effective business manager with considerable energy and drive and proven ability to develop new business ventures. Quickly grasps new ideas and establishes priorities to develop sound plans to maximise existing resources and to ensure effective results.
- **Man Management**
  Decisive leader with strong motivational skills and a participative style of management who encourages contribution from all levels of staff.
- **Communication**
  Persuasive communicator and effective listener at all levels. Highly developed verbal and written presentation abilities.
- **Sales, Marketing and Trading**
  Powerful sales negotiator, at main board level, resulting in profitable, large UK and international deals. Secures long term business contracts by establishing ongoing client relationships. Successfully assesses and develops new products and markets.
- **Sales, Marketing and Trading**
  Powerful sales negotiator, at main board level, resulting in profitable, large UK and international deals. Secures long term business contracts by establishing ongoing client relationships. Successfully assesses and develops new products and markets.

QUALIFICATIONS

Reading University 1979 - 1982
BA (Hons) 2(ii) Economics & Geography
Warwick School 1972 - 1979
8 'O' levels; 4 'A' levels

CAREER HISTORY

March 1992 to present:

International Trader

T W Steel & Company Ltd – Coryton
Trading House with turnover of £15 million.
Planned and set up new division in timber
trading serving the Caribbean market. Main
achievements:
– Quickly determined market requirements
   and how this could be served. Identified
   and initiated support required by agents.
– Selected, developed and motivated agents
   to sell this new product line effectively.
– Assessed and selected suppliers based
   on quality, reliability and commitment.
– Generated sales to establish this new
   division.

May 1985 to Mar 1992:

Director, 1988–1992

Juno Products Ltd – Hamwood
Large Agency house with turnover in 1991
of 25 million.
Prime responsibilities to negotiate with
suppliers, manage UK sales force and
support staff and control finance. Main
achievements:
– Agency agreements secured resulting in
   additional turnover from the Philippines
   of £6 million in 1990 and from Chile of
   £1.5 million in 1991.
– Expanded sales over the period 1989–1991
   by 25%.
– Established clear leadership of team which
   led to a significant increase in motivation
   and enthusiasm which directly contributed
   to improved results.

Salesman, 1985–1988

Successfully increased customer base by 20%
and turnover by 25% with maintained margins
over the period 1985–1988.

Aug 1982–May 1985:

Salesman

John Jackson plc – London
Sizeable independent Timber Importer with
turnover in 1985 of £50 million

Main achievements:
– Expanded volume and profitability by 30%
within 18 months.
– Promoted new product range. Rapid
increase in turnover to £1.5 million led to a
separate company being formed within the
group.

OTHER RELEVANT INFORMATION

Completed management courses, external and in-house covering sales,
marketing, sales management, presentation and public speaking.
Regularly lectured to TRADA.

ROGER REYNOLDS
25 The Place, London W1N 3ZZ
Phone: 001 95 9617   DOB 23.11.65

A dynamic, enthusiastic and well motivated individual with a strong sense of integrity. Very much a team player functioning effectively in groups in a supporting, motivating or leadership role. Operates consistently well under pressure, is entrepreneurially spirited with a desire for a continually challenging and demanding environment to express full potential and total commitment to excellence. Possesses finely honed administrative and organisational skills and an ability to communicate easily and effectively with individuals or groups at all levels. Being highly perceptive and objective is able to quickly identify that which will make a positive difference in a situation and act appropriately.

EXPERIENCE AND ACHIEVEMENTS

Aug 91–Feb 93   Self Employed Communication Consultant in Monaco

This included work with The International Institute improving office administration structures, installing time management systems and coaching staff on personal effectiveness and inter-office communications, resulting in a significant increase in available billable hours for the Consultants.

Jan 91–Aug 91   Various appointments in the Leisure Industry

Successfully managed a large ski chalet in the French Alps for Lunar Travel and worked in a service capacity on luxury motor yachts on the French Riviera.

Nov 89–Jan 91   Various self employed projects

Independent Distributor for a new health and beauty product marketing organisation, Holly International. Within two months was recognised as a key player by the Marketing Director and was offered free office space within the company headquarters.

Project Director for Charity organisation. Initiated, developed and ran a new organisation aimed at encouraging young people to actively participate, in their own way, in the goals of the Charity. Concurrently led and managed an extraordinary project designed to end the civil war in Ethiopia. The project was hugely successful and generated participation from over 65,000 young people throughout 14 countries, support from many celebrities and establishment figures, and 70+ articles of media coverage by press, radio and television.

Apr 89–Nov 89   Graduate Trainee Consultant with Worldwide Consulting

Main area of activity was systems programming and basic system design within customized client information systems. Having been selected from the top 2% of University graduates, continued to achieve results during training and regular assessment placing me at the top end of my graduate intake.

Jun 88–Apr 89　　**Various projects undertaken whilst awaiting start date with Worldwide Consulting**

Resort Representative for Apres Ski Club in the French Alps. Responsible for the organisation and entertainment of groups of up to 120 students, achieving 'most active and popular rep' by the end of the season.

Consultant Engineer in an African Development Project in Arusha, Tanzania. The project offered early and invaluable exposure to the management of change in confronting and awkward situations.

Oct 85–Jun 88　　**Printon University studying Mining Engineering**

As well as running 2 university clubs, participating on the committee of 2 others and playing for both the university squash and karate teams. Achieved a first class degree and the highest final results in the department year.

Sep 84–Oct 85　　**Student Mine Official with Deep Mining Corp, South Africa**

Gained hands on experience in gold, coal and diamond mines and at the age of 19 learned how to successfully manage a 30 strong team of native African miners.

Sep 77–Jun 84　　**Oldtown Grammar School**

Achieved 4 'A' levels and 9 'O' levels, played on the squash, football, cricket, swimming and athletic teams, was awarded the prize of 'Victor Ludorum' for the student contributing the most to the junior school, won the senior debating prize, held the highest rank in the school cadet force and was nominated Head Boy.

Other Qualifications

Extensive computing knowledge including programming and file handling and proficiency in many word processing, spreadsheet and draw packages. Speak and read French.

Interests and Sports

Professionally instructed squash, snow skiing and snow boarding, aerobics/calisthenics and Yoga. Participate in most forms of water sport and have studied, practised and taught various martial and healing arts. A passion for communication, relationship and global issues and a love for travel, having visited or lived in 20+ countries in the last 8 years, including trekking 70 miles across the Himalayas with no guide and very little food and surviving naturally for 4 weeks on an uninhabited tropical island.

Also Available from Kogan Page

Career Counselling for Executives, Godfrey Golzen
Getting There: Jobhunting for Women (2nd edition),
  Margaret Wallis
*Great Answers to Tough Interview Questions: How to Get the
  Job You Want* (3rd edition), Martin John Yate
How to Get A Job after 45, Julie Bayley
Job Sharing: A Practical Guide, Pam Walton
*The Mid-Career Action Guide: A Practical Guide to Mid Career
  Change* (2nd edition), Derek Kemp and Fred Kemp
Moving Up: A Practical Guide to Career Advancement,
  Stan Crabtree
Offbeat Careers: 60 Ways to Avoid Becoming an Accountant,
  (2nd edition), Vivien Donald
Portable Careers: How to Survive Your Partner's Relocation,
  Linda R Greenbury
*Working Abroad: The Daily Telegraph Guide to Working and
  Living Overseas* (15th edition), Godfrey Golzen
Your Employment Rights, Michael Malone